ENCYCLICAL LETTER
SOLLICITUDO REI SOCIALIS
OF THE SUPREME PONTIFF
JOHN PAUL II
TO THE BISHOPS
PRIESTS
RELIGIOUS FAMILIES
SONS AND DAUGHTERS OF THE CHURCH
AND ALL PEOPLE OF GOOD WILL
FOR THE TWENTIETH ANNIVERSARY OF
POPULORUM PROGRESSIO

CONTENTS

I.   Introduction 3

II. Originality of the Encyclical *Populorum Progressio* 8

III. Survey of the contemporary world . 19

IV. Authentic human development . . 47

V.   A theological reading of modern problems 67

VI. Some particular guidelines . . . 81

VII. Conclusion 92

Venerable Brothers

and dear Sons and Daughters,

Health and the Apostolic Blessing!

I
INTRODUCTION

1. THE SOCIAL CONCERN of the Church, directed towards an authentic development of man and society which would respect and promote all the dimensions of the human person, has always expressed itself in the most varied ways. In recent years, one of the special means of intervention has been the Magisterium of the Roman Pontiffs which, beginning with the Encyclical *Rerum Novarum* of Leo XIII as a point of reference,[1] has frequently dealt with the question and has sometimes made the dates of publication of the various social docu-

---

[1] Leo XIII, Encyclical *Rerum Novarum* (15 May 1891): *Leonis XIII P.M. Acta*, XI, Romae 1892, pp. 97-144.

ments coincide with the anniversaries of that first document.[2]

The Popes have not failed to throw fresh light by means of those messages upon new aspects of the social doctrine of the Church. As a result, this doctrine, beginning with the outstanding contribution of Leo XIII and enriched by the successive contributions of the Magisterium, has now become an updated doctrinal "corpus". It builds up gradually, as the Church, in the fullness of the word revealed by Christ Jesus[3] and with the assistance of the Holy Spirit (cf. *Jn* 14:16, 26; 16:13-15), reads events as they unfold in the course of history. She thus seeks to lead people to respond, with the support also of rational reflection and of the human sciences, to their vocation as responsible builders of earthly society.

2. Part of this large body of social teaching is the distinguished Encyclical *Populorum Progressio*[4] which my esteemed predecessor Paul VI published on 26 March 1967.

---

[2] Pius XI, Encyclical *Quadragesimo Anno* (15 May 1931): *AAS* 23 (1931), pp. 177-228; John XXIII, *Encyclical Mater et Magistra* (15 May 1961): *AAS* 53 (1961), pp. 401-464; Paul VI, Apostolic Letter *Octogesima Adveniens* (14 May 1971): *AAS* 63 (1971), pp. 401-441; John Paul II, Encyclical *Laborem Exercens* (14 September 1981): *AAS* 73 (1981), pp. 577-647. Also Pius XII delivered a radio message (1 June 1941) for the fiftieth anniversary of the Encyclical of Leo XIII: *AAS* 33 (1941), pp. 195-205.

[3] C. Second Vatican Ecumenical Council, Dogmatic Constitution on Divine Revelation *Dei Verbum*, 4.

[4] Paul VI, Encyclical *Populorum Progressio* (26 March 1967): *AAS* 59 (1967), pp. 257-299.

The enduring relevance of this Encyclical is easily recognized if we note the series of commemorations which took place during 1987 in various forms and in many parts of the ecclesiastical and civil world. For this same purpose, the Pontifical Commission *Iustitia et Pax* sent a circular letter to the Synods of the Oriental Catholic Churches and to the Episcopal Conferences, asking for ideas and suggestions on the best way to celebrate the Encyclical's anniversary, to enrich its teachings and, if need be, to update them. At the time of the twentieth anniversary, the same Commission organized a solemn commemoration in which I myself took part and gave the concluding address.[5] And now, also taking into account the replies to the above-mentioned circular letter, I consider it appropriate, at the close of the year 1987, to devote an Encyclical to the theme of *Populorum Progressio*.

3. In this way I wish principally to achieve *two objectives* of no little importance: on the one hand, to pay homage to this historic document of Paul VI and to its teaching; on the other hand, following in the footsteps of my esteemed predecessors in the See of Peter, to reaffirm the *continuity* of the social doctrine as well as its constant *renewal*. In effect, continuity and renewal are a proof of the *perennial value* of the teaching of the Church.

[5] Cf. *L'Osservatore Romano*, 25 May 1987.

This twofold dimension is typical of her teaching in the social sphere. On the one hand it is *constant,* for it remains identical in its fundamental inspiration, in its "principles of reflection", in its "criteria of judgment", in its basic "directives for action",[6] and above all in its vital link with the Gospel of the Lord. On the other hand, it is ever *new,* because it is subject to the necessary and opportune adaptations suggested by the changes in historical conditions and by the unceasing flow of the events which are the setting of the life of people and society.

4. I am convinced that the teachings of the Encyclical *Populorum Progressio,* addressed to the people and the society of the sixties, retain all their force as an *appeal to conscience* today in the last part of the eighties, in an effort to trace the major lines of the present world always within the context of the aim and inspiration of the "development of peoples", which are still very far from being exhausted. I therefore propose to extend the impact of that message by bringing it to bear, with its possible applications, upon the present historical moment, which is no less dramatic than that of twenty years ago.

As we well know, time maintains a constant and unchanging rhythm. Today however we

---

[6] Cf. CONGREGATION FOR THE DOCTRINE OF THE FAITH, Instruction on Christian Freedom and Liberation *Libertatis Conscientia* (22 March 1986), 72: *AAS* 79 (1987), p. 586; PAUL VI, Apostolic Letter *Octogesima Adveniens* (14 May 1971), 4: *AAS* 63 (1971), pp. 403 f.

have the impression that it is passing *ever more quickly,* especially by reason of the multiplication and complexity of the phenomena in the midst of which we live. Consequently, the *configuration of the world* in the course of the last twenty years, while preserving certain fundamental constants, has undergone notable changes and presents some totally new aspects.

The present period of time, on the eve of the third Christian millennium, is characterized by a widespread expectancy, rather like a new "Advent",[7] which to some extent touches everyone. It offers an opportunity to study the teachings of the Encyclical in greater detail and to see their possible future developments.

The aim of the present *reflection* is to emphasize, through a theological investigation of the present world, the need for a fuller and more nuanced concept of development, according to the suggestions contained in the Encyclical. Its aim is also to indicate some ways of putting it into effect.

---

[7] Cf. Encyclical *Redemptoris Mater* (25 March 1987), 3: *AAS* 79 (1987), pp. 363 f.; Homily at the Mass of 1 January 1987: *L'Osservatore Romano,* 2 January 1987.

II

ORIGINALITY OF THE ENCYCLICAL
POPULORUM PROGRESSIO

5.   As soon as it appeared, the document of
Pope Paul VI captured the attention of public
opinion by reason of its *originality*. In a concrete
manner and with great clarity, it was possible
to identify the above-mentioned characteristics
of *continuity* and *renewal* within the Church's
social doctrine. The intention of rediscovering
numerous aspects of this teaching, through a
careful re-reading of the Encyclical, will therefore constitute the main thread of the present
reflections.

   But first I wish to say a few words about
the *date* of publication: the year 1967. The
very fact that Pope Paul VI chose to publish
a *social Encyclical* in that year invites us to
consider the document in relationship to the
Second Vatican Ecumenical Council, which had
ended on 8 December 1965.

6.   We should see something more in this than
simple chronological *proximity*. The Encyclical

Populorum Progressio presents itself, in a certain way, as *a document which applies the teachings of the Council.* It not only makes continual reference to the texts of the Council,[8] but it also flows from the same concern of the Church which inspired the whole effort of the Council —and in a particular way the Pastoral Constitution *Gaudium et Spes*—to coordinate and develop a number of themes of her social teaching.

We can therefore affirm that the Encyclical *Populorum Progressio* is a kind of response to the *Council's appeal* with which the Constitution *Gaudium et Spes* begins: "The joys and the hopes, the griefs and the anxieties of the people of this age, especially those who are poor or in any way afflicted, these too are the joys and hopes, the griefs and anxieties of the followers of Christ. Indeed, nothing genuinely human fails to raise an echo in their hearts".[9] These words express the *fundamental motive* inspiring the great document of the Council, which begins by noting the situation of *poverty* and of *underdevelopment* in which millions of human beings live.

This *poverty* and *underdevelopment* are, under another name, the "griefs and the anxieties" of today, of "especially those who are

---

[8] The Encyclical *Populorum Progressio* cites the documents of the Second Vatican Ecumenical Council nineteen times, and sixteen of the references are to the Pastoral Constitution on the Church in the Modern World *Gaudium et Spes*.

[9] *Gaudium et Spes*, 1.

poor". Before this vast panorama of pain and suffering the Council wished to suggest horizons of joy and hope. The Encyclical of Paul VI has the same purpose, in full fidelity to the inspiration of the Council.

7. There is also the *theme* of the Encyclical which, in keeping with the great tradition of the Church's social teaching, takes up again in a direct manner the *new exposition* and *rich synthesis* which the Council produced, notably in the Constitution *Gaudium et Spes.*

With regard to the content and themes once again set forth by the Encyclical, the following should be emphasized: the awareness of the duty of the Church, as "an expert in humanity", "to scrutinize the signs of the times and to interpret them in the light of the Gospel"; [10] the awareness, equally profound, of her mission of "service", a mission distinct from the function of the State, even when she is concerned with people's concrete situation; [11] the reference to the notorious inequalities in the situations of those same people; [12] the confirmation of the Council's teaching, a faithful echo of the centuries-old tradition of the Church, regarding the "universal

[10] *Ibid.,* 4; cf. *Populorum Progressio* 13: *loc. cit.,* p. 263, 264.
[11] Cf. *Gaudium et Spes,* 3; *Populorum Progressio,* 13: *loc. cit.,* p. 264.
[12] Cf. *Gaudium et Spes,* 63; *Populorum Progressio,* 9: *loc. cit.,* p. 269.

purpose of goods"; [13] the appreciation of the culture and the technological civilization which contribute to human liberation, [14] without failing to recognize their limits; [15] finally, on the specific theme of development, which is precisely the theme of the Encyclical, the insistence on the "most serious duty" incumbent on the more developed nations "to help the developing countries". [16] The same idea of development proposed by the Encyclical flows directly from the approach which the Pastoral Constitution takes to this problem. [17]

These and other explicit references to the Pastoral Constitution lead one to conclude that the Encyclical presents itself as an *application* of the Council's teaching in social matters to the specific problem of the *development* and the *underdevelopment of peoples.*

8.   This brief analysis helps us to appreciate better the *originality* of the Encyclical, which can be stated in *three* points.

The *first* is constituted by the *very fact* of a document, issued by the highest authority of

---

[13] Cf. *Gaudium et Spes,* 69; *Populorum Progressio,* 22: loc. cit., p. 269.

[14] Cf. *Gaudium et Spes,* 57; *Populorum Progressio,* 41: loc. cit., p. 277.

[15] Cf. *Gaudium et Spes,* 19; *Populorum Progressio,* 41: loc. cit., pp. 277 f.

[16] Cf. *Gaudium et Spes,* 86; *Populorum Progressio,* 48: loc. cit., p. 281.

[17] Cf. *Gaudium et Spes,* 69; *Populorum Progressio,* 14-21: loc. cit., pp. 264-268.

the Catholic Church and addressed both to the Church herself and "to all people of good will",[18] on a matter which at first sight is solely *economic* and *social:* the *development* of peoples. The term "development" is taken from the vocabulary of the social and economic sciences. From this point of view, the Encyclical *Populorum Progressio* follows directly in the line of the Encyclical *Rerum Novarum,* which deals with the "condition of the workers".[19] Considered superficially, both themes could seem extraneous to the legitimate concern of the Church seen as a *religious institution*—and "development" even more so than the "condition of the workers".

In continuity with the Encyclical of Leo XIII, it must be recognized that the document of Paul VI possesses the merit of having emphasized the *ethical* and *cultural character* of the problems connected with development, and likewise the legitimacy and necessity of the Church's intervention in this field.

In addition, the social doctrine of the Church has once more demonstrated its character as an *application* of the word of God to people's lives and the life of society, as well as to the earthly realities connected with them, offering "princi-

---

[18] Cf. The *Inscriptio* of the Encyclical *Populorum Progressio: loc. cit.,* p. 257.

[19] The Encyclical *Rerum Novarum* of Leo XIII has as its principal subject "the condition of the workers": *Leonis XIII P.M. Acta,* XI, Romae 1892, p. 97.

ples for reflection", "criteria of judgment" and "directives for action".[20] Here, in the document of Paul VI, one finds these three elements with a prevalently practical orientation, that is, directed towards *moral conduct*.

In consequence, when the Church concerns herself with the "development of peoples", she cannot be accused of going outside her own specific field of competence and, still less, outside the mandate received from the Lord.

9.   The *second* point of *originality* of *Populorum Progressio* is shown by the *breadth of outlook* open to what is commonly called the "social question".

In fact, the Encyclical *Mater et Magistra* of Pope John XXIII had already entered into this wider outlook [21] and the Council had echoed the same in the Constitution *Gaudium et Spes*.[22] However, the social teaching of the Church had not yet reached the point of affirming with such clarity that the social question has acquired a worldwide dimension,[23] nor had this affirmation and the accompanying analysis yet been made

[20] Cf. CONGREGATION FOR THE DOCTRINE OF THE FAITH, Instruction on Christian Freedom and Liberation *Libertatis Conscientia* (22 March 1986), 72: *AAS* 79 (1987), p. 586; PAUL VI, Apostolic Letter *Octogesima Adveniens* (14 May 1971), 4: *AAS* 63 (1971), pp. 403 f.

[21] Cf. Encyclical *Mater et Magistra* (15 May 1961): *AAS* 53 (1961), p. 440.

[22] *Gaudium et Spes*, 63.

[23] Cf. Encyclical *Populorum Progressio*, 3: *loc. cit.*, p. 258; cf. also *ibid.*, 9: *loc. cit.*, p. 261.

into a "directive for action", as Paul VI did in his Encyclical.

Such an explicit taking up of a position offers a *great wealth* of content, which it is appropriate to point out.

In the first place a *possible misunderstanding* has to be eliminated. Recognition that the "social question" has assumed a worldwide dimension does not at all mean that it has lost its *incisiveness* or its national and local importance. On the contrary, it means that the problems in industrial enterprises or in the workers' and union movements of a particular country or region are not to be considered as isolated cases with no connection. On the contrary they depend more and more on the influence of factors beyond regional boundaries and national frontiers.

Unfortunately, from the economic point of view, the developing countries are much more numerous than the developed ones; the multitudes of human beings who lack the goods and services offered by development are *much more numerous* than those who possess them.

We are therefore faced with a serious problem of *unequal distribution* of the means of subsistence originally meant for everybody, and thus also an unequal distribution of the benefits deriving from them. And this happens not through the *fault* of the needy people, and even less through a sort of *inevitability* dependent on natural conditions or circumstances as a whole.

The Encyclical of Paul VI, in declaring that the social question has acquired worldwide dimensions, first of all points out a *moral fact,* one which has its foundation in an objective analysis of reality. In the words of the Encyclical itself, "each one must be conscious" of this fact,[24] precisely because it directly concerns the conscience, which is the source of moral decisions.

In this framework, the *originality* of the Encyclical consists not so much in the affirmation, historical in character, of the universality of the social question, but rather in the *moral evaluation* of this reality. Therefore political leaders, and citizens of rich countries considered as individuals, especially if they are Christians, have *the moral obligation,* according to the degree of each one's responsibility, to *take into consideration,* in personal decisions and decisions of government, this relationship of universality, this interdependence which exists between their conduct and the poverty and underdevelopment of so many millions of people. Pope Paul's Encyclical translates more succinctly the moral obligation as the "duty of solidarity";[25] and this affirmation, even though many situations have changed in the world, has the same force and validity today as when it was written.

On the other hand, without departing from the lines of this moral vision, the *originality* of

[24] Cf. *ibid.,* 3: *loc. cit.,* p. 258.
[25] *Ibid.,* 48: *loc. cit.,* p. 281.

the Encyclical also consists in the basic insight that the *very concept* of development, if considered in the perspective of universal interdependence, changes notably. True development *cannot* consist in the simple accumulation of wealth and in the greater availability of goods and services, if this is gained at the expense of the development of the masses, and without due consideration for the social, cultural and spiritual dimensions of the human being.[26]

10. As a *third point,* the Encyclical provides a very original contribution to the social doctrine of the Church in its totality and to the very concept of development. This originality is recognizable in a phrase of the document's concluding paragraph and which can be considered as its summary, as well as its historic label: "Development is the new name for peace".[27]

In fact, if the social question has acquired a worldwide dimension, this is because *the demand for justice* can only be satisfied on that level. To ignore this demand could encourage the temptation among the victims of injustice to respond with violence, as happens at the origin of many wars. Peoples excluded from the fair distribution of the goods originally

---

[26] Cf. *ibid.,* 14: *loc. cit.,* p. 264: "Development cannot be limited to mere economic growth. In order to be authentic, it must be complete: integral, that is, it has to promote the good of every man and of the whole man".

[27] *Ibid.,* 87: *loc. cit.,* p. 299.

destined for all could ask themselves: why not respond with violence to those who first treat us with violence? And if the situation is examined in the light of the division of the world into ideological blocs—a division already existing in 1967—and in the light of the subsequent economic and political repercussions and dependencies, the danger is seen to be much greater.

The first consideration of the striking content of the Encyclical's historic phrase may be supplemented by a second consideration to which the document itself alludes: [28] how can one justify the fact that *huge sums of money,* which could and should be used for increasing the development of peoples, are instead utilized for the enrichment of individuals or groups, or assigned to the increase of stockpiles of weapons, both in developed countries and in the developing ones, thereby upsetting the real priorities? This is even more serious given the difficulties which often hinder the direct transfer of capital set aside for helping needy countries. If "development is the new name for peace", war and military preparations are the major enemy of the integral development of peoples.

In the light of this expression of Pope Paul VI, we are thus invited to re-examine the *concept of development.* This of course is not limited to merely satisfying material necessities

[28] Cf. *ibid.,* 53: *loc. cit.,* p. 283.

through an increase of goods, while ignoring the sufferings of the many and making the selfishness of individuals and nations the principal motivation. As the Letter of Saint James pointedly reminds us: "What causes wars, and what causes fightings among you? Is it not your passions that are at war in your members? You desire and do not have" (*Js* 4: 1-2).

On the contrary, in a different world, ruled by concern for the *common good* of all humanity, or by concern for the "spiritual and human development of all" instead of by the quest for individual profit, peace would be *possible* as the result of a "more perfect justice among people".[29]

Also this new element of the Encyclical has a *permanent and contemporary value,* in view of the modern attitude which is so sensitive to the close link between respect for justice and the establishment of real peace.

[29] Cf. *ibid.,* 76: *loc. cit.,* p. 295.

III

SURVEY
OF THE CONTEMPORARY WORLD

11.   In its own time *the fundamental teaching* of the Encyclical *Populorum Progressio* received great acclaim for its novel character. The social context in which we live today cannot be said to be completely *identical* to that of twenty years ago. For this reason, I now wish to conduct a brief review of some of the characteristics of today's world, in order to develop the teaching of Paul VI's Encyclical, once again from the point of view of the "development of peoples".

12.   *The first fact* to note is that the *hopes for development,* at that time so lively, today appear very far from being realized.

In this regard, the Encyclical had no illusions. Its language, grave and at times dramatic, limited itself to stressing the seriousness of the situation and to bringing before the conscience of all the urgent obligation of contributing to its solution. In those years there was a *certain* widespread *optimism* about the possibility of overcoming, without excessive efforts, the economic backwardness of the poorer peoples, of providing them with infrastructures and assisting them in the process of industrialization.

In that historical context, over and above the efforts of each country, the United Nations Organization promoted consecutively *two decades of development*.[30] In fact, some measures, bilateral and multilateral, were taken with the aim of helping many nations, some of which had already been independent for some time, and others—the majority—being States just born from the process of decolonization. For her part, the Church felt the duty to deepen her understanding of the problems posed by the new situation, in the hope of supporting these efforts with her religious and human inspiration, in order to give them a "soul" and an effective impulse.

13. It cannot be said that these various religious, human, economic and technical initiatives have been in vain, for they have succeeded in achieving certain results. But in general, taking into account the various factors, one cannot deny that the present situation of the world, from the point of view of development, offers a *rather negative* impression.

For this reason, I wish to call attention to a number of *general indicators,* without excluding other specific ones. Without going into an analy-

---

[30] The decades referred to are the years 1960-1970 and 1970-1980; the present decade is the third (1980-1990).

sis of figures and statistics, it is sufficient to face squarely the reality of an *innumerable multitude of people*—children, adults and the elderly—in other words, real and unique human persons, who are suffering under the intolerable burden of poverty. There are many millions who are deprived of hope due to the fact that, in many parts of the world, their situation has noticeably worsened. Before these tragedies of total indigence and need, in which so many of *our brothers and sisters* are living, it is the Lord Jesus himself who comes to question us (cf. *Mt* 25: 31-46).

14. The first *negative observation* to make is the persistence and often the widening of the *gap* between the areas of the so-called developed North and the developing South. This geographical terminology is only indicative, since one cannot ignore the fact that the frontiers of wealth and poverty intersect within the societies themselves, whether developed or developing. In fact, just as social inequalities down to the level of poverty exist in rich countries, so, in parallel fashion, in the less developed countries one often sees manifestations of selfishness and a flaunting of wealth which is as disconcerting as it is scandalous.

The abundance of goods and services available in some parts of the world, particularly in the developed North, is matched in the South by an unacceptable delay, and it is precisely in this geopolitical area that the major part of the human race lives.

Looking at all the various sectors—the production and distribution of foodstuffs, hygiene, health and housing, availability of drinking water, working conditions (especially for women), life expectancy and other economic and social indicators—the general picture is a disappointing one, both considered in itself and in relation to the corresponding data of the more developed countries. The word "gap" returns spontaneously to mind.

Perhaps this is not the appropriate word for indicating the true reality, since it could give the impression of a *stationary* phenomenon. This is not the case. The *pace of progress* in the developed and developing countries in recent years has differed, and this serves to widen the distances. Thus the developing countries, especially the poorest of them, find themselves in a situation of very serious delay.

We must also add the *differences of culture* and *value systems* between the various population groups, differences which do not always match the degree of *economic development,* but which help to create distances. These are elements and aspects which render *the social question much more complex,* precisely because this question has assumed a universal dimension.

As we observe the various parts of the world separated by this widening gap, and note that each of these parts seems to follow its own path with its own achievements, we can understand the current usage which speaks of different worlds within our *one world:* the First World, the Second World, the Third World and at times the Fourth World.[31] Such expressions, which obviously do not claim to classify exhaustively all countries, are significant: they are a sign of a widespread sense that the *unity of the world,* that is, *the unity of the human race,* is seriously compromised. Such phraseology, beyond its more or less objective value, undoubtedly conceals a *moral content,* before which the Church, which is a "sacrament or sign and instrument ... of the unity of the whole human race",[32] cannot remain indifferent.

15.   However, the picture just given would be incomplete if one failed to add to the "economic and social indices" of underdevelopment other indices which are equally negative and indeed even more disturbing, beginning with the cultural level. These are *illiteracy,* the difficulty or impossibility of obtaining *higher education,* the inability to share in the *building of one's own nation,* the *various forms of exploitation* and of economic, social, political and even religious *oppression* of the individual and his or

---

[31] The expression "Fourth World" is used not just occasionally for the so-called *less advanced* countries, but also and especially for the bands of great or extreme poverty in countries of medium and high income.

[32] SECOND VATICAN ECUMENICAL COUNCIL, Dogmatic Constitution on the Church *Lumen Gentium,* 1.

23

her rights, *discrimination of every type,* especially the exceptionally odious form based on difference of race. If some of these scourges are noted with regret in areas of the more developed North, they are undoubtedly more frequent, more lasting and more difficult to root out in the developing and less advanced countries.

It should be noted that in today's world, among other rights, *the right of economic initiative* is often suppressed. Yet it is a right which is important not only for the individual but also for the common good. Experience shows us that the denial of this right, or its limitation in the name of an alleged "equality" of everyone in society, diminishes, or in practice absolutely destroys the spirit of initiative, that is to say *the creative subjectivity of the citizen.* As a consequence, there arises, not so much a true equality as a "levelling down". In the place of creative initiative there appears passivity, dependence and submission to the bureaucratic apparatus which, as the only "ordering" and "decision-making" body—if not also the "owner"—of the entire totality of goods and the means of production, puts everyone in a position of almost absolute dependence, which is similar to the traditional dependence of the worker-proletarian in capitalism. This provokes a sense of frustration or desperation and predisposes people to opt out of national life, impelling many to emigrate and also favouring a form of "psychological" emigration.

Such a situation has its consequences also from the point of view of the "rights of individual nations". In fact, it often happens that a nation is deprived of its subjectivity, that is to say the "sovereignty" which is its right, in its economic, political-social and in a certain way cultural significance, since in a national community all these dimensions of life are bound together.

It must also be restated that no social group, for example a political party, has the right to usurp the role of sole leader, since this brings about the destruction of the true subjectivity of society and of the individual citizens, as happens in every form of totalitarianism. In this situation the individual and the people become "objects", in spite of all declarations to the contrary and verbal assurances.

We should add here that in today's world there are many other *forms of poverty*. For are there not certain privations or deprivations which deserve this name? The denial or the limitation of human rights—as for example the right to religious freedom, the right to share in the building of society, the freedom to organize and to form unions, or to take initiatives in economic matters—do these not impoverish the human person as much as, if not more than, the deprivation of material goods? And is development which does not take into account the full affirmation of these rights really development on the human level?

In brief, modern underdevelopment is not only economic but also cultural, political and simply human, as was indicated twenty years ago by the Encyclical *Populorum Progressio.* Hence at this point we have to ask ourselves if the sad reality of today might not be, at least in part, the result of a *too narrow idea* of development, that is, a mainly economic one.

16.   It should be noted that in spite of the praiseworthy efforts made in the last two decades by the more developed or developing nations and the International Organizations to find a way out of the situation, or at least to remedy some of its symptoms, the conditions have become *notably worse.*

Responsibility for this deterioration is due to various causes. Notable among them are undoubtedly grave instances of omissions on the part of the developing nations themselves, and especially on the part of those holding economic and political power. Nor can we pretend not to see the responsibility of the developed nations, which have not always, at least in due measure, felt the duty to help countries separated from the affluent world to which they themselves belong.

Moreover, one must denounce the existence of economic, financial and social *mechanisms* which, although they are manipulated by people, often function almost automatically, thus accentuating the situation of wealth for some and poverty for the rest. These mechanisms, which are manoeuvred directly or indirectly by the more developed countries, by their very functioning favour the interests of the people manipulating them. But in the end they suffocate or condition the economies of the less developed countries. Later on these mechanisms will have to be subjected to a careful analysis under the ethical-moral aspect.

Populorum Progressio already foresaw the possibility that under such systems the wealth of the rich would increase and the poverty of the poor would remain.[33] A proof of this forecast has been the appearance of the so-called Fourth World.

17.   However much society worldwide shows signs of fragmentation, expressed in the conventional names First, Second, Third and even Fourth World, their *interdependence* remains close. When this interdependence is separated from its ethical requirements, it has *disastrous consequences* for the weakest. Indeed, as a result of a sort of internal dynamic and under the impulse of mechanisms which can only be called perverse, this *interdependence* triggers *negative effects* even in the rich countries. It is precisely within these countries that one encounters, though on a lesser scale, the *more specific manifestations* of underdevelopment.

---

[33] Encyclical *Populorum Progressio*, 33: *loc. cit.*, p. 273.

Thus it should be obvious that development either becomes shared in *common* by every part of the world or it undergoes a *process of regression* even in zones marked by constant progress. This tells us a great deal about the nature of *authentic* development: either *all* the nations of the world participate, or it will not be true development.

Among the *specific signs* of underdevelopment which increasingly affect the developed countries also, there are two in particular that reveal a tragic situation. The *first* is the *housing crisis*. During this International Year of the Homeless proclaimed by the United Nations, attention is focused on the millions of human beings lacking adequate housing or with no housing at all, in order to awaken everyone's conscience and to find a solution to this serious problem with its negative consequences for the individual, the family and society.[34]

The lack of housing is being experienced *universally* and is due in large measure to the growing phenomenon of urbanization.[35] Even the most highly developed peoples present the sad spectacle of individuals and families literally struggling to survive, without a *roof* over their

[34] It should be noted that the Holy See associated itself with the celebration of this International Year with a special Document issued by the Pontifical Commission "Iustitia et Pax" entitled "What Have You Done to Your Homeless Brother?" - *The Church and the Housing Problem* (27 December 1987).

[35] Cf. PAUL VI, Apostolic Letter *Octogesima Adveniens* (14 May 1971), 8-9: *AAS* 63 (1971), pp. 406-408.

heads or with a roof *so inadequate* as to constitute no roof at all.

The lack of housing, an extremely serious problem in itself, should be seen as a sign and summing-up of a whole series of shortcomings, economic, social, cultural or simply human in nature. Given the extent of the problem, we should need little convincing of how far we are from an authentic development of peoples.

18.   *Another indicator* common to the vast majority of nations is the phenomenon of *unemployment* and *underemployment*.

Everyone recognizes the *reality* and *growing seriousness* of this problem in the industrialized countries.[36] While it is alarming in the developing countries, with their high rate of population growth and their large numbers of young people, in the countries of high economic development the *sources of work* seem to be shrinking, and thus the opportunities for employment are decreasing rather than increasing.

This phenomenon too, with its series of negative consequences for individuals and for society, ranging from humiliation to the loss of that self-respect which every man and woman should have, prompts us to question seriously

---

[36] A recent United Nations publication entitled *World Economic Survey 1987* provides the most recent data (cf. pp. 8-9). The percentage of unemployed in the developed countries with a market economy jumped from 3% of the work force in 1970 to 8% in 1986. It now amounts to 29 million people.

the type of development which has been followed over the past twenty years. Here the words of the Encyclical *Laborem Exercens* are extremely appropriate: "It must be stressed that the constitutive element in this *progress* and also the most adequate *way to verify it* in a spirit of justice and peace, which the Church proclaims and for which she does not cease to pray... is *the continual reappraisal of man's work,* both in the aspect of its objective finality and in the aspect of the dignity of the subject of all work, that is to say, man". On the other hand, "we cannot fail to be struck by *a disconcerting fact* of immense proportions: the fact that ... there are huge numbers of people who are unemployed ... a fact that without any doubt demonstrates that both within the individual political communities and in their relationships on the continental and world level there is something wrong with the organization of work and employment, precisely at the most critical and socially most important points".[37]

This second phenomenon, like the previous one, because it is *universal* in character and tends to *proliferate,* is a very telling negative sign of the state and the quality of the development of peoples which we see today.

19.   A *third phenomenon,* likewise characteristic of the most recent period, even though it

[37] Encyclical Letter *Laborem Exercens* (14 September 1981), 18: *AAS* 73 (1981), pp. 624-625.

is not met with everywhere, is without doubt equally indicative of the *interdependence* between developed and less developed countries. It is the question of the *international debt*, concerning which the Pontifical Commission "Iustitia et Pax" has issued a document.[38]

At this point one cannot ignore the *close connection* between a problem of this kind—the growing seriousness of which was already foreseen in *Populorum Progressio* [39]—and the question of the development of peoples.

The reason which prompted the developing peoples to accept the offer of abundantly available capital was the hope of being able to invest it in development projects. Thus the availability of capital and the fact of accepting it as a loan can be considered a contribution to development, something desirable and legitimate in itself, even though perhaps imprudent and occasionally hasty.

Circumstances having changed, both within the debtor nations and in the international financial market, the instrument chosen to make a contribution to development has turned into

[38] *At the Service of the Human Community: An Ethical Approach to the International Debt Question* (27 December 1986).

[39] Encyclical Letter *Populorum Progressio*, 54: *loc. cit.*, pp. 283 f: "Developing countries will thus no longer risk being overwhelmed by debts whose repayment swallows up the greater part of their gains. Rates of interest and time for repayment of the loan could be so arranged as not to be too great a burden on either party, taking into account free gifts, interest-free or low-interest loans, and the time needed for liquidating the debts".

a *counter-productive mechanism.* This is because the debtor nations, in order to service their debt, find themselves obliged to export the capital needed for improving or at least maintaining their standard of living. It is also because, for the same reason, they are unable to obtain new and equally essential financing.

Through this mechanism, the means intended for the development of peoples has turned into a *brake* upon development instead, and indeed in some cases has even *aggravated underdevelopment.*

As the recent document of the Pontifical Commission "Iustitia et Pax" states,[40] these observations should make us reflect on the *ethical character* of the interdependence of peoples. And along similar lines, they should make us reflect on the requirements and conditions, equally inspired by ethical principles, for cooperation in development.

20. If at this point we examine the *reasons* for this serious delay in the process of development, a delay which has occurred contrary to the indications of the Encyclical *Populorum Progressio,* which had raised such great hopes, our attention is especially drawn to the *political* causes of today's situation.

[40] Cf. "Presentation" of the document *At the Service of the Human Community: An Ethical Approach to the International Debt Question* (27 December 1986).

Faced with a combination of factors which are undoubtedly complex, we cannot hope to achieve a comprehensive analysis here. However, we cannot ignore a striking fact about the *political picture* since the Second World War, a fact which has considerable impact on the forward movement of the development of peoples.

I am referring to the *existence of two opposing blocs,* commonly known as the East and the West. The reason for this description is not purely political but is also, as the expression goes, *geopolitical.* Each of the two blocs tends to assimilate or gather around it other countries or groups of countries, to different degrees of adherence or participation.

The opposition is first of all *political,* inasmuch as each bloc identifies itself with a system of organizing society and exercising power which presents itself as an alternative to the other. The political opposition, in turn, takes its origin from a deeper opposition which is *ideological* in nature.

In the West there exists a system which is historically inspired by the principles of the *liberal capitalism* which developed with industrialization during the last century. In the East there exists a system inspired by the *Marxist collectivism* which sprang from an interpretation of the condition of the proletarian classes made in the light of a particular reading of history. Each of the two ideologies, on the basis of two very different visions of man and of his freedom and social role, has proposed and still promotes, on the economic level, antithetical forms of the organization of labour and of the structures of ownership, especially with regard to the so-called means of production.

It was inevitable that by developing antagonistic systems and centres of power, each with its own forms of propaganda and indoctrination, the *ideological opposition* should evolve into a growing *military opposition* and give rise to two blocs of armed forces, each suspicious and fearful of the other's domination.

International relations, in turn, could not fail to feel the effects of this "logic of blocs" and of the respective "spheres of influence". The tension between the two blocs which began at the end of the Second World War has dominated the whole of the subsequent forty years. Sometimes it has taken the form of *"cold war"*, sometimes of *"wars by proxy"*, through the manipulation of local conflicts, and sometimes it has kept people's minds in suspense and anguish by the threat of an *open and total* war.

Although at the present time this danger seems to have receded, yet without completely disappearing, and even though an initial agreement has been reached on the destruction of one type of nuclear weapon, the existence and opposition of the blocs continue to be a real and worrying fact which still colours the world picture.

21.   This happens with particularly negative effects in the international relations which concern the developing countries. For as we know the tension *between East and West* is not in itself an opposition between two different *levels* of development but rather between two *concepts* of the development of individuals and peoples, both concepts being imperfect and in need of radical correction. This opposition is transferred to the developing countries themselves, and thus helps to widen the gap already existing on the economic level between *North and South* and which results from the distance between the two *worlds:* the more developed one and the less developed one.

This is one of the reasons why the Church's social doctrine adopts a critical attitude towards both liberal capitalism and Marxist collectivism. For from the point of view of development the question naturally arises: in what way and to what extent are these two systems capable of changes and updatings such as to favour or promote a true and integral development of individuals and peoples in modern society? In fact, these changes and updatings are urgent and essential for the cause of a development common to all.

Countries which have recently achieved independence, and which are trying to establish a cultural and political identity of their own, and need effective and impartial aid from all the richer and more developed countries, find themselves involved in, and sometimes overwhelmed by, ideological conflicts, which inevitably create internal divisions, to the extent in some cases of provoking full civil war. This is also because investments and aid for development are often diverted from their proper purpose and used to sustain conflicts, apart from and in opposition to the interests of the countries which ought to benefit from them. Many of these countries are becoming more and more aware of the danger of falling victim to a form of neo-colonialism and are trying to escape from it. It is this awareness which in spite of difficulties, uncertainties and at times contradictions gave rise to the *International Movement of Non-Aligned Nations,* which, in its positive aspect, would like to affirm in an effective way the right of every people to its own identity, independence and security, as well as the right to share, on a basis of equality and solidarity, in the goods intended for all.

22.　In the light of these considerations, we easily arrive at a clearer picture of the last twenty years and a better understanding of the conflicts in the northern hemisphere, namely between East and West, as an important cause of the retardation or stagnation of the South.

The developing countries, instead of becoming *autonomous nations* concerned with their own progress towards a just sharing in the goods and services meant for all, become parts of a machine, cogs on a gigantic wheel. This is often true also in the field of social communications, which, being run by centres mostly in the northern hemisphere, do not always give due consideration to the priorities and problems of such countries or respect their cultural make-up. They frequently impose a distorted vision of life and of man, and thus fail to respond to the demands of true development.

Each of the two *blocs* harbours in its own way a tendency towards *imperialism,* as it is usually called, or towards forms of neo-colonalism: an easy temptation to which they frequently succumb, as history, including recent history, teaches.

It is this abnormal situation, the result of a war and of an unacceptably exaggerated concern *for security,* which deadens the impulse towards united cooperation by all for the common good of the human race, to the detriment especially of peaceful peoples who are impeded from their rightful access to the goods meant for all.

Seen in this way, the present division of the world is a *direct obstacle* to the real transformation of the conditions of underdevelopment in the developing and less advanced countries. However, peoples do not always resign themselves to their fate. Furthermore, the very needs of an economy stifled by military expenditure and by bureaucracy and intrinsic inefficiency now seem to favour processes which might mitigate the existing opposition and make it easier to begin a fruitful dialogue and genuine collaboration for peace.

23. The statement in the Encyclical *Populorum Progressio* that the resources and investments devoted to arms production ought to be used to alleviate the misery of impoverished peoples [41] makes more urgent the appeal to overcome the opposition between the two blocs.

Today, the reality is that these resources are used to enable each of the two blocs to overtake the other and thus guarantee its own security. Nations which historically, economically and politically have the possibility of playing a leadership role are prevented by this fundamentally flawed distortion from adequately fulfilling their duty of solidarity for the benefit of peoples which aspire to full development.

It is timely to mention—and it is no exaggeration—that a leadership role among nations can only be justified by the possibility and willingness to contribute widely and generously to the common good.

If a nation were to succumb more or less deliberately to the temptation to close in upon itself and failed to meet the responsibilities following from its superior position in the community of nations, it *would fall seriously short* of its clear ethical duty. This is readily apparent in the circumstances of history, where believers

[41] Cf. Encyclical Letter *Populorum Progressio*, 53; *loc. cit.*, p. 283.

discern the dispositions of Divine Providence, ready to make use of the nations for the realization of its plans, so as to render "vain the designs of the peoples" (cf. *Ps* 33/32:10).

When the West gives the impression of abandoning itself to forms of growing and selfish isolation, and the East in its turn seems to ignore for questionable reasons its duty to cooperate in the task of alleviating human misery, then we are up against not only a betrayal of humanity's legitimate expectations—a betrayal that is a harbinger of unforeseeable consequences—but also a real desertion of a moral obligation.

24.   If arms production is a serious disorder in the present world with regard to true human needs and the employment of the means capable of satisfying those needs, *the arms trade* is equally to blame. Indeed, with reference to the latter it must be added that the *moral judgment is even more severe.* As we all know, this is a trade without frontiers, capable of crossing even the barriers of the blocs. It knows how to overcome the division between East and West, and above all the one between North and South, to the point—and this is more serious—of pushing its way into the *different sections* which make up the southern hemisphere. We are thus confronted with a strange phenomenon: while economic aid and development plans meet with the obstacle of insuperable ideological barriers, and with tariff and trade barriers, *arms* of whatever

origin circulate with almost total freedom all over the world. And as the recent document of the Pontifical Commission "Iustitia et Pax" on the international debt points out,[42] everyone knows that in certain cases the capital lent by the developed world has been used in the under-developed world to buy weapons.

If to all this we add the *tremendous* and universally acknowledged *danger* represented by *atomic weapons* stockpiled on an incredible scale, the logical conclusion seems to be this: in today's world, including the world of econo-mics, the prevailing picture is one destined to lead us more quickly *towards death* rather than one of concern for *true development* which would lead all towards a "more human" life, as en-visaged by the Encyclical *Populorum Progressio.*[43]

The consequences of this state of affairs are to be seen in the festering of a *wound* which typifies and reveals the imbalances and conflicts of the modern world: *the millions of refugees* whom war, natural calamities, persecution and discrimination of every kind have deprived of home, employment, family and homeland. The tragedy of these multitudes is reflected in the hopeless faces of men, women and children who can no longer find a home in a divided and inhospitable world.

[42] *At the Service of the Human Community: An Ethical Approach to the International Debt Question* (27 December 1986), III, 2, 1.

[43] Cf. Encyclical Letter *Populorum Progressio*, 20-21: *loc. cit.,* pp. 267 f.

Nor may we close our eyes to another painful wound in today's world: the phenomenon of *terrorism,* understood as the intention to kill people and destroy property indiscriminately, and to create a climate of terror and insecurity, often including the taking of hostages. Even when some ideology or the desire to create a better society is adduced as the motivation for this inhuman behaviour, acts of terrorism are never justifiable. Even less so when, as happens today, such decisions and such actions, which at times lead to real massacres, and to the abduction of innocent people who have nothing to do with the conflicts, claim to have a propaganda purpose for furthering a cause. It is still worse when they are an end in themselves, so that murder is committed merely for the sake of killing. In the face of such horror and suffering, the words I spoke some years ago are still true, and I wish to repeat them again: "What Christianity forbids is to seek solutions ... by the ways of hatred, by the murdering of defenceless people, by the methods of terrorism".[44]

25. At this point something must be said about the *demographic problem* and the way it is spoken of today, following what Paul VI said in his Encyclical [45] and what I myself stated at

[44] Address at Drogheda, Ireland (29 September 1979), 5: *AAS* 71 (1979), II, p. 1079.
[45] Cf. Encyclical Letter *Populorum Progressio,* 37: *loc. cit.,* pp. 275 f.

41

length in the Apostolic Exhortation *Familiaris Consortio.*[46]

One cannot deny the existence, especially in the southern hemisphere, of a demographic problem which creates difficulties for development. One must immediately add that in the northern hemisphere the nature of this problem is reversed: here, the cause for concern is the *drop in the birthrate,* with repercussions on the aging of the population, unable even to renew itself biologically. In itself, this is a phenomenon capable of hindering development. Just as it is incorrect to say that such difficulties stem solely from demographic growth, neither is it proved that *all* demographic growth is incompatible with orderly development.

On the other hand, it is very alarming to see governments in many countries launching *systematic campaigns* against birth, contrary not only to the cultural and religious identity of the countries themselves but also contrary to the nature of true development. It often happens that these campaigns are the result of pressure and financing coming from abroad, and in some cases they are made a condition for the granting of financial and economic aid and assistance. In any event, there is an *absolute lack of respect* for the freedom of choice of the parties involved, men and women often subjected to intolerable

---

[46] Cf. Apostolic Exhortation *Familiaris Consortio* (22 November 1981), especially in 30: *AAS* 74 (1982), pp. 115-117.

pressures, including economic ones, in order to force them to submit to this new form of oppression. It is the poorest populations which suffer such mistreatment, and this sometimes leads to a tendency towards a form of racism, or the promotion of certain equally racist forms of eugenics.

This fact too, which deserves the most forceful condemnation, is a *sign* of an erroneous and perverse *idea* of true human development.

26. This mainly negative overview of the *actual situation* of development in the contemporary world would be incomplete without a mention of the coexistence of *positive aspects*.

The *first* positive note is the *full awareness* among large numbers of men and women of their own dignity and of that of every human being. This awareness is expressed, for example, in the more *lively concern* that *human rights should be respected,* and in the more vigorous rejection of their violation. One sign of this is the number of recently established private associations, some worldwide in membership, almost all of them devoted to monitoring with great care and commendable objectivity what is happening *internationally* in this sensitive field.

At this level one must acknowledge the *influence* exercised by the *Declaration of Human Rights,* promulgated some forty years ago by the United Nations Organization. Its very existence and gradual acceptance by the international community are signs of a growing awareness. The same is to be said, still in the field of human rights, of other juridical instruments issued by the United Nations Organization or other International Organizations.[47]

The awareness under discussion applies not only to *individuals* but also to *nations* and *peoples,* which, as entities having a specific cultural identity, are particularly sensitive to the preservation, free exercise and promotion of their precious heritage.

At the same time, in a world divided and beset by every type of conflict, the *conviction* is growing of a radical *interdependence* and consequently of the need for a solidarity which will take up interdependence and transfer it to the moral plane. Today perhaps more than in the past, people are realizing that they are linked together by a *common destiny,* which is to be constructed together, if catastrophe for all is to be avoided. From the depth of anguish, fear and escapist phenomena like drugs, *typical of the contemporary world,* the idea is slowly emerging that the good to which we are all called and the happiness to which we aspire cannot be obtained without an *effort and commitment on the part of all,* nobody excluded, and the consequent renouncing of personal selfishness.

[47] Cf. Human Rights. Collection of International Instruments, United Nations, New York 1983; John Paul II, Encyclical Letter *Redemptor Hominis* (4 March 1979), 17: *AAS* 71 (1979), p. 296.

Also to be mentioned here, as a sign of *respect for life*—despite all the temptations to destroy it by abortion and euthanasia—is a *concomitant concern* for peace, together with an awareness that peace is *indivisible*. It is either *for all* or *for none*. It demands an ever greater degree of rigorous respect for *justice* and consequently a fair distribution of the results of true development.[48]

Among today's *positive signs* we must also mention a greater realization of the limits of available resources, and of the need to respect the integrity and the cycles of nature and to take them into account when planning for development, rather than sacrificing them to certain demagogic ideas about the latter. Today this is called *ecological concern*.

It is also right to acknowledge the generous commitment of statesmen, politicians, economists, trade unionists, people of science and international officials—many of them inspired by religious faith—who at no small personal sacrifice try to resolve the world's ills and who give of themselves in every way so as to ensure that an

---

[48] Cf. SECOND VATICAN ECUMENICAL COUNCIL, Pastoral Constitution on the Church in the Modern World *Gaudium et Spes*, 78; PAUL VI, Encyclical Letter *Populorum Progressio*, 76: *loc. cit.*, pp. 294 f.: "To wage war on misery and to struggle against injustice is to promote, along with improved conditions, the human and spiritual progress of all men, and therefore the common good of humanity ... peace is something that is built up day after day, in the pursuit of an order intended by God, which implies a more perfect form of justice among men".

ever increasing number of people may enjoy the benefits of peace and a quality of life worthy of the name.

The great *International Organizations,* and a number of the Regional Organizations, *contribute* to this *in no small measure.* Their united efforts make possible more effective action.

It is also through these contributions that some Third World countries, despite the burden of many negative factors, have succeeded in reaching a *certain self-sufficiency in food,* or a degree of industrialization which makes it possible to survive with dignity and to guarantee sources of employment for the active population.

Thus, *all is not negative* in the contemporary world, nor could it be, for the Heavenly Father's Providence lovingly watches over even our daily cares (cf. *Mt* 6:25-32; 10:23-31; *Lk* 12:6-7; 22-30). Indeed, the positive values which we have mentioned testify to a new moral concern, particularly with respect to the great human problems such as development and peace.

This fact prompts me to turn my thoughts to the *true nature* of the development of peoples, along the lines of the Encyclical which we are commemorating, and as a mark of respect for its teaching.

IV

AUTHENTIC HUMAN DEVELOPMENT

27. The examination which the Encyclical invites us to make of the contemporary world leads us to note in the first place that developmen *is not* a straightforward process, *as it were automatic* and *in itself limitless,* as though, given certain conditions, the human race were able to progress rapidly towards an undefined perfection of some kind.[49]

Such an idea — linked to a notion of "progress" with philosophical connotations deriving from the Enlightenment, rather than to the notion of "development"[50] which is used in a specifically economic and social sense — now seems to be seriously called into doubt, particularly since the tragic experience of the two world wars, the planned and partly achieved destruction of whole peoples, and the looming

---

[49] Cf. Apostolic Exhortation *Familiaris Consortio* (22 November 1981), 6: *AAS* 74 (1982), p. 88: "...history is not simply a fixed progression towards what is better, but rather an event of freedom, and even a struggle between freedoms ...".

[50] For this reason the word "development" was used in the Encyclical rather than the word "progress", but with an attempt to give the word "development" its fullest meaning.

atomic peril. A naive *mechanistic optimism* has been replaced by a well-founded anxiety for the fate of humanity.

28.   At the same time, however, the "*economic*" concept itself, linked to the word development, has entered into crisis. In fact there is a better understanding today that the *mere accumulation* of goods and services, even for the benefit of the majority, is not enough for the realization of human happiness. Nor, in consequence, does the availability of the many *real benefits* provided in recent times by science and technology, including the computer sciences, bring freedom from every form of slavery. On the contrary, the experience of recent years shows that unless all the considerable body of resources and potential at man's disposal is guided by a *moral understanding* and by an orientation towards the true good of the human race, it easily turns against man to oppress him.

A *disconcerting conclusion* about the most recent period should serve to enlighten us: side-by-side with the miseries of underdevelopment, themselves unacceptable, we find ourselves up against a form of *superdevelopment,* equally inadmissible, because like the former it is contrary to what is good and to true happiness. This superdevelopment, which consists in an *excessive* availability of every kind of material goods for the benefit of certain social groups, easily makes people slaves of "possession" and of immediate gratification, with no other horizon than the multiplication or continual replacement of the things already owned with others still better. This is the so-called civilization of "consumption" or "consumerism", which involves so much "throwing-away" and "waste". An object already owned but now superseded by something better is discarded, with no thought of its possible lasting value in itself, nor of some other human being who is poorer.

All of us experience firsthand the sad effects of this blind submission to pure consumerism: in the first place a crass materialism, and at the same time a *radical dissatisfaction,* because one quickly learns—unless one is shielded from the flood of publicity and the ceaseless and tempting offers of products—that the more one possesses the more one wants, while deeper aspirations remain unsatisfied and perhaps even stifled.

The Encyclical of Pope Paul VI pointed out the difference, so often emphasized today, between "having" and "being",[51] which had been expressed earlier in precise words by the Second

---

[51] Encyclical Letter *Populorum Progressio,* 19, *loc. cit.,* pp. 266 f.: "Increased possession is not the ultimate goal of nations or of individuals. All growth is ambivalent ... The exclusive pursuit of possessions thus becomes an obstacle to individual fulfilment and to man's true greatness ... both for nations and for individual men, avarice is the most evident form of moral underdevelopment"; cf. also PAUL VI, Apostolic Letter *Octogesima Adveniens* (14 May 1971), 9: *AAS* 63 (1971), pp. 407 f.

Vatican Council.[52] To "have" objects and goods does not in itself perfect the human subject, unless it contributes to the maturing and enrichment of that subject's "being", that is to say unless it contributes to the realization of the human vocation as such.

Of course, the difference between "being" and "having", the danger inherent in a mere multiplication or replacement of things possessed compared to the value of "being", need not turn into a *contradiction*. One of the greatest injustices in the contemporary world consists precisely in this: that the ones who possess much are relatively *few* and those who possess almost nothing are *many*. It is the injustice of the poor distribution of the goods and services originally intended for all.

This then is the picture: there are some people—the few who possess much—who do not really succeed in "being" because, through a reversal of the hierarchy of values, they are hindered by the cult of "having"; and there are others—the many who have little or nothing— who do not succeed in realizing their basic human vocation because they are deprived of essential goods.

The evil does not consist in "having" as such, but in possessing without regard for the *quality* and the *ordered hierarchy* of the goods

---

[52] Cf. Pastoral Constitution on the Church in the Modern World *Gaudium et Spes,* 35; PAUL VI, Address to the Diplomatic Corps (7 January 1965): *AAS* 57 (1965), p. 232.

one has. *Quality and hierarchy* arise from the subordination of goods and their availability to man's "being" and his true vocation.

This shows that although *development* has a *necessary economic dimension,* since it must supply the greatest possible number of the world's inhabitants with an availability of goods essential for them "to be", it is not limited to that dimension. If it is limited to this, then it turns against those whom it is meant to benefit.

The characteristics of full development, one which is "more human" and able to sustain itself at the level of the true vocation of men and women without denying economic requirements, were described by Paul VI.[53]

29.   Development which is not only economic must be measured and oriented according to the reality and vocation of man seen in his totality, namely, according to his *interior dimension.* There is no doubt that he needs created goods and the products of industry, which is constantly being enriched by scientific and technological progress. And the ever greater availability of material goods not only meets needs but also opens new horizons.   The danger of the misuse of material goods and the appearance of artificial needs should in no way hinder the regard we have for the new goods and resources placed at our disposal and the use we make of them.   On the

[53] Cf. Encyclical Letter *Populorum Progressio,* 20-21: *loc. cit.,* pp. 267 f.

contrary, we must see them as a gift from God and as a response to the human vocation, which is fully realized in Christ.

However, in trying to achieve true development we must never lose sight of that *dimension* which is in the *specific nature* of man, who has been created by God in his image and likeness (cf. *Gen* 1:26). It is a bodily and a spiritual nature, symbolized in the second creation account by the two elements: the *earth,* from which God forms man's body, and the *breath of life* which he breathes into man's nostrils (cf. *Gen* 2:7).

Thus man comes to have a certain affinity with other creatures: he is called to use them, and to be involved with them. As the Genesis account says (cf. *Gen* 2:15), he is placed in the garden with the duty of cultivating and watching over it, being superior to the other creatures placed by God under his dominion (cf. *Gen* 1:25-26). But at the same time man must remain subject to the will of God, who imposes limits upon his use and dominion over things (cf. *Gen* 2:16-17), just as he promises him immortality (cf. *Gen* 2:9; *Wis* 2:23). Thus man, being the image of God, has a true affinity with him too.

On the basis of this teaching, development cannot consist only in the use, dominion over and *indiscriminate* possession of created things and the products of human industry, but rather in *subordinating* the possession, dominion and use to man's divine likeness and to his vocation to immortality. This is the *transcendent reality* of the human being, a reality which is seen to be shared from the beginning by a couple, a man and a woman (cf. *Gen* 1:27), and is therefore fundamentally social.

30.   According to Sacred Scripture therefore, the notion of development is not only "lay" or "profane", but is also seen to be, while having a socio-economic dimension of its own, the *modern expression* of an essential dimension of man's vocation.

The fact is that man was not created, so to speak, immobile and static. The first portrayal of him, as given in the Bible, certainly presents him as a *creature* and *image, defined* in his deepest reality by the *origin* and *affinity* that constitute him. But all this plants within the human being—man and woman—the *seed* and the *requirement* of a special task to be accomplished by each individually and by them as a couple. The task is "to have dominion" over the other created beings, "to cultivate the garden". This is to be accomplished within the framework of *obedience* to the divine law and therefore with respect for the image received, the image which is the clear foundation of the power of dominion recognized as belonging to man as the means to his perfection (cf. *Gen* 1:26-30; 2:15-16; *Wis* 9:2-3).

When man disobeys God and refuses to submit to his rule, nature rebels against him and no longer recognizes him as its "master", for he has tarnished the divine image in himself. The claim to ownership and use of created things remains still valid, but after sin its exercise becomes difficult and full of suffering (cf. *Gen* 3:17-19).

In fact, the following chapter of *Genesis* shows us that the descendants of Cain build "a city", engage in sheep farming, practise the arts (music) and technical skills (metallurgy); while at the same time people began to "call upon the name of the Lord" (cf. *Gen* 4:17-26).

The story of the human race described by Sacred Scripture is, even after the fall into sin, a story of *constant achievements,* which, although always called into question and threatened by sin, are nonetheless repeated, increased and extended in response to the divine vocation given from the beginning to man and to woman (cf. *Gen* 1:26-28) and inscribed in the image which they received.

It is logical to conclude, at least on the part of those who believe in the word of God, that today's "development" is to be seen as a moment in the story which began at creation, a story which is constantly endangered by reason of infidelity to the Creator's will, and especially by the temptation to idolatry. But this "development" fundamentally corresponds to the first premises. Anyone wishing to renounce the *difficult yet noble task* of improving the lot of man in his totality, and of all people, with the excuse that the struggle is difficult and that constant effort is required, or simply because of the experience of defeat and the need to begin again, that person would be betraying the will of God the Creator. In this regard, in the Encyclical *Laborem Exercens* I referred to man's vocation to work, in order to emphasize the idea that it is always man who is the protagonist of development.[54]

Indeed, the Lord Jesus himself, in the parable of the talents, emphasizes the severe treatment given to the man who dared to hide the gift received: "You wicked and slothful servant! You knew that I reap where I have not sowed and gather where I have not winnowed? ... So take the talent from him, and give it to him who has the ten talents" (*Mt* 25:26-28). It falls to us, who receive the gifts of God in order to make them fruitful, to "sow" and "reap". If we do not, even what we have will be taken away from us.

A deeper study of these harsh words will make us commit ourselves more resolutely to the *duty,* which is urgent for everyone today, to work together for the full development of others: "development of the whole human being and of all people".[55]

---

[54] Cf. Encyclical Letter *Laborem Exercens* (14 September 1981), 4: *AAS* 73 (1981), pp. 584 f.; PAUL VI, Encyclical Letter *Populorum Progressio,* 15: *loc. cit.,* p. 265.

[55] Encyclical Letter *Populorum Progressio,* 42: *loc. cit.,* p. 278.

31. *Faith in Christ the Redeemer,* while it illuminates from within the nature of development, also guides us in the task of collaboration. In the Letter of Saint Paul to the Colossians, we read that Christ is "the firstborn of all creation", and that "all things were created through him" and for him (1:15-16). In fact, "all things hold together in him", since "in him all the fullness of God was pleased to dwell, and through him to reconcile to himself all things (v. 20).

A part of this divine plan, which begins from eternity in Christ, the perfect "image" of the Father, and which culminates in him, "the firstborn from the dead" (v. 18), *is our own history,* marked by our personal and collective effort to raise up the human condition and to overcome the obstacles which are continually arising along our way. It thus prepares us to share in the fullness which "dwells in the Lord" and which he communicates "to his body, which is the Church" (v. 18; cf. *Eph* 1:22-23). At the same time sin, which is always attempting to trap us and which jeopardizes our human achievements, is conquered and redeemed by the "reconciliation" accomplished by Christ (cf. *Col.* 1:20).

Here the perspectives widen. The dream of "unlimited progress" reappears, radically transformed by the *new outlook* created by Christian faith, assuring us that progress is possible only because God the Father has decided from the beginning to make man a sharer of his glory in Jesus Christ risen from the dead, in whom "we have redemption through his blood ... the forgiveness of our trespasses" (*Eph* 1: 7). In him God wished to conquer sin and make it serve our greater good,[56] which infinitely surpasses what progress could achieve.

We can say therefore—as we struggle amidst the obscurities and deficiencies of *underdevelopment* and *superdevelopment*—that one day this corruptible body will put on incorruptibility, this mortal body immortality (cf. *1 Cor* 15: 54), when the Lord "delivers the Kingdom to God the Father" (v. 24) and all the works and actions that are worthy of man will be redeemed.

Furthermore, the concept of faith makes quite clear the reasons which impel the *Church* to concern herself with the problems of development, to consider them a *duty of her pastoral ministry,* and to urge all to think about the nature and characteristics of authentic human development. Through her commitment she desires, on the one hand, to place herself at the service of the divine plan which is meant to order all things to the fullness which dwells in Christ (cf. *Col* 1: 19) and which he communicated to his body; and on the other hand she desires to respond to her fundamental voca-

---

[56] Cf. *Praeconium Paschale, Missale Romanum,* ed. typ. altera, 1975, p. 272: "O certe necessarium Adae peccatum, quod Christi morte deletum est! O felix culpa, quae talem ac tantum meruit habere Redemptorem!".

tion of being a "sacrament", that is to say "a sign and instrument of intimate union with God and of the unity of the whole human race".[57]

Some Fathers of the Church were inspired by this idea to develop in original ways a concept of the *meaning of history* and of *human work,* directed towards a goal which surpasses this meaning and which is always defined by its relationship to the work of Christ. In other words, one can find in the teaching of the Fathers an *optimistic vision* of history and work, that is to say of the *perennial value* of authentic human achievements, inasmuch as they are redeemed by Christ and destined for the promised Kingdom.[58]

Thus, part of the *teaching* and most ancient *practice* of the Church is her conviction that she is obliged by her vocation—she herself, her ministers and each of her members—to relieve the misery of the suffering, both far and near, not only out of her "abundance" but also out of her "necessities". Faced by cases of need, one cannot ignore them in favour of superfluous church ornaments and costly furnishings for divine worship; on the contrary it could be obligatory to sell these goods in order to provide

[57] SECOND VATICAN ECUMENICAL COUNCIL, Dogmatic Constitution on the Church *Lumen Gentium,* 1.

[58] Cf. for example, St Basil the Great, *Regulae fusius tractatae, interrogatio* XXXVII, 1-2: *PG* 31, 1009-1012; Theodoret of Cyr, *De Providentia, Oratio* VII: *PG* 83, 665-686; St Augustine, *De Civitate Dei,* XIX, 17: *CCL* 48, 683-685.

food, drink, clothing and shelter for those who lack these things.[59] As has been already noted, here we are shown a "*hierarchy of values*"—in the framework of the right to property—between "having" and "being", especially when the "having" of a few can be to the detriment of the "being" of many others.

In his Encyclical Pope Paul VI stands in the line of this teaching, taking his inspiration from the Pastoral Constitution *Gaudium et Spes*.[60] For my own part, I wish to insist once more on the seriousness and urgency of that teaching, and I ask the Lord to give all Christians the strength to put it faithfully into practice.

32. The obligation to commit oneself to the development of peoples is not just an *individual* duty, and still less an *individualistic* one, as if it were possible to achieve this development through the isolated efforts of each individual.

---

[59] Cf. for example, St JOHN CHRYSOSTOM, *In Evang. S. Matthaei, hom.* 50, 3-4: *PG* 58, 508-510; St Ambrose, *De Officiis Ministrorum,* lib. II, XXVIII, 136-140: *PL* 16, 139-141; St Possidius, *Vita S. Augustini Episcopi,* XXIV: *PL* 32, 53 f.

[60] Encyclical Letter *Populorum Progressio,* 23: *loc. cit.,* p. 268: " 'If someone who has the riches of this world sees his brother in need and closes his heart to him, how does the love of God abide in him?' (1 Jn 3:17). It is well known how strong were the words used by the Fathers of the Church to describe the proper attitude of persons who possess anything towards persons in need". In the previous number, the Pope had cited No. 69 of the Pastoral Constitution *Gaudium et Spes* of the Second Vatican Ecumenical Council.

It is an imperative which obliges *each and every* man and woman, as well as societies and nations. In particular, it obliges the Catholic Church and the other Churches and Ecclesial Communities, with which we are completely willing to collaborate in this field. In this sense, just as we Catholics invite our Christian brethren to share in our initiatives, so too we declare that we are ready to collaborate in theirs, and we welcome the invitations presented to us. In this pursuit of integral human development we can also do much with the members of other religions, as in fact is being done in various places.

Collaboration in the development of the whole person and of every human being is in fact a duty *of all towards all,* and must be shared by the four parts of the world: East and West, North and South; or, as we say today, by the different "worlds". If, on the contrary, people try to achieve it in only one part, or in only one world, they do so at the expense of the others; and, precisely because the others are ignored, their own development becomes exaggerated and misdirected.

Peoples or *nations* too have a right to their own full development, which while including —as already said—the economic and social aspects should also include individual cultural identity and openness to the transcendent. Not even the need for development can be used as an excuse for imposing on others one's own way of life or own religious belief.

33.   Nor would a type of development which did not respect and promote *human rights*—personal and social, economic and political, including the *rights of nations and of peoples*—be really *worthy of man.*

Today, perhaps more than in the past, the *intrinsic contradiction* of a development limited *only* to its economic element is seen more clearly. Such development easily subjects the human person and his deepest needs to the demands of economic planning and selfish profit.

The *intrinsic connection* between authentic development and respect for human rights once again reveals the *moral* character of development: the true elevation of man, in conformity with the natural and historical vocation of each individual, is not attained *only* by exploiting the abundance of goods and services, or by having available perfect infrastructures.

When individuals and communities do not see a rigorous respect for the moral, cultural and spiritual requirements, based on the dignity of the person and on the proper identity of each community, beginning with the family and religious societies, then all the rest—availability of goods, abundance of technical resources applied to daily life, a certain level of material well-being—will prove unsatisfying and in the end contemptible. The Lord clearly says this in the

Gospel, when he calls the attention of all to the true hierarchy of values: "For what will it profit a man, if he gains the whole world and forfeits his life?" (*Mt* 16:26).

True development, in keeping with the *specific* needs of the human being—man or woman, child, adult or old person—implies, especially for those who actively share in this process and are responsible for it, a lively *awareness* of the *value* of the rights of all and of each person. It likewise implies a lively awareness of the need to respect the right of every individual to the full use of the benefits offered by science and technology.

On the *internal level* of every nation, respect for all rights takes on great importance, especially: the right to life at every stage of its existence; the rights of the family, as the basic social community, or "cell of society"; justice in employment relationships; the rights inherent in the life of the political community as such; the rights based on the *transcendent vocation* of the human being, beginning with the right of freedom to profess and practise one's own religious belief.

On the *international level,* that is, the level of relations between States or, in present-day usage, between the different "worlds", there must be complete *respect* for the identity of each people, with its own historical and cultural characteristics. It is likewise essential, as the

Encyclical *Populorum Progressio* already asked, to recognize each people's equal right "to be seated at the table of the common banquet",[61] instead of lying outside the door like Lazarus, while "the dogs come and lick his sores" (cf. *Lk* 16:21). Both peoples and individuals must enjoy the *fundamental equality*[62] which is the basis, for example, of the Charter of the United Nations Organization: the equality which is the basis of the right of all to share in the process of full development.

In order to be genuine, development must be achieved within the framework of *solidarity* and *freedom,* without ever sacrificing either of them under whatever pretext. The moral character of development and its necessary promotion are emphasized when the most rigorous respect is given to all the demands deriving from the order of *truth* and *good* proper to the human person. Furthermore the Christian who is taught to see that man is the image of God, called to share in the truth and the good which

[61] Cf. Encyclical Letter *Populorum Progressio,* 47: "... a world where freedom is not an empty word and where the poor man Lazarus can sit down at the same table with the rich man".

[62] Cf. *ibid.,* 47: "It is a question, rather, of building a world where every man, no matter what his race, religion or nationality, can live a fully human life, freed from servitude imposed on him by other men ..."; cf. also SECOND VATICAN ECUMENICAL COUNCIL, Pastoral Constitution on the Church in the Modern World *Gaudium et Spes,* 29. Such *fundamental equality* is one of the basic reasons why the Church has always been opposed to every form of racism.

is *God himself,* does not understand a commitment to development and its application which excludes regard and respect for the unique dignity of this "image". In other words, true development must be based on the *love of God and neighbour,* and must help to promote the relationships between individuals and society. This is the "civilization of love" of which Paul VI often spoke.

34.   Nor can the moral character of development exclude respect *for the beings which constitute* the natural world, which the ancient Greeks—alluding precisely to the *order* which distinguishes it—called the "cosmos". Such realities also demand respect, by virtue of a threefold consideration which it is useful to reflect upon carefully.

The *first* consideration is the appropriateness of acquiring a *growing awareness* of the fact that one cannot use with impunity the different categories of beings, whether living or inanimate —animals, plants, the natural elements—simply as one wishes, according to one's own economic needs.   On the contrary, one must take into account *the nature of each being* and of its *mutual connection* in an ordered system, which is precisely the "cosmos".

The *second consideration* is based on the realization—which is perhaps more urgent— that *natural resources* are limited; some are not, as it is said, *renewable*. Using them as if they were inexhaustible, with *absolute dominion,* seriously endangers their availability not only for the present generation but above all for generations to come.

The *third consideration* refers directly to the consequences of a certain type of development on the *quality of life* in the industrialized zones. We all know that the direct or indirect result of industrialization is, ever more frequently, the pollution of the environment, with serious consequences for the health of the population.

Once again it is evident that development, the planning which governs it, and the way in which resources are used must include respect for moral demands. One of the latter undoubtedly imposes limits on the use of the natural world. The dominion granted to man by the Creator is not an absolute power, nor can one speak of a freedom to "use and misuse", or to dispose of things as one pleases. The limitation imposed from the beginning by the Creator himself and expressed symbolically by the prohibition not to "eat of the fruit of the tree" (cf. *Gen* 2:16-17) shows clearly enough that, when it comes to the natural world, we are subject not only to biological laws but also to moral ones, which cannot be violated with impunity.

A true concept of development cannot ignore the use of the elements of nature, the renewability of resources and the consequences of haphazard industrialization—three considerations which alert our consciences to the *moral dimension* of development.[63]

---

[63] Cf. Homily at Val Visdende (12 July 1987), 5: *L'Osservatore Romano,* 13-14 July 1987; PAUL VI, Apostolic Letter *Octogesima Adveniens* (14 May 1971), 21: *AAS* 63 (1971), pp. 416 f.

V

A THEOLOGICAL READING
OF MODERN PROBLEMS

35. Precisely because of the essentially moral character of development, it is clear that the *obstacles* to development likewise have a moral character. If in the years since the publication of Pope Paul's Encyclical there has been no development—or very little, irregular, or even contradictory development—the reasons are not only economic. As has already been said, political motives also enter in. For the decisions which either accelerate or slows down the development of peoples are really political in character. In order to overcome the misguided mechanisms mentioned earlier and to replace them with new ones which will be more just and in conformity with the common good of humanity, an effective political will is needed. Unfortunately, after analyzing the situation we have to conclude that this political will has been insufficient.

In a document of a pastoral nature such as this, an analysis limited exclusively to the economic and political causes of underdevelopment (and, *mutatis mutandis,* of so-called super-development) would be incomplete. It is therefore necessary to single out the *moral* causes which, with respect to the behaviour of *individuals* considered as *responsible persons,* interfere in such a way as to slow down the course of development and hinder its full achievement.

Similarly, when the scientific and technical resources are available which, with the necessary concrete political decisions, ought to help lead peoples to true development, the main obstacles to development will be overcome only by means of *essentially moral decisions.* For believers, and especially for Christians, these decisions will take their inspiration from the principles of faith, with the help of divine grace.

36.   It is important to note therefore that a world which is divided into blocs, sustained by rigid ideologies, and in which instead of interdependence and solidarity different forms of imperialism hold sway, can only be a world subject to structures of sin. The sum total of the negative factors working against a true awareness of the universal *common good,* and the need to further it, gives the impression of creating, in persons and institutions, an obstacle which is difficult to overcome.[64]

[64] Cf. SECOND VATICAN ECUMENICAL COUNCIL, Pastoral Constitution on the Church in the Modern World *Gaudium et Spes,* 25.

If the present situation can be attributed to difficulties of various kinds, it is not out of place to speak of "structures of sin", which, as I stated in my Apostolic Exhortation *Reconciliatio et Paenitentia,* are rooted in personal sin, and thus always linked to the *concrete acts* of individuals who introduce these structures, consolidate them and make them difficult to remove.[65] And thus they grow stronger, spread, and become the source of other sins, and so influence people's behaviour.

"Sin" and "structures of sin" are categories which are seldom applied to the situation of the contemporary world. However, one cannot easily gain a profound understanding of the reality that confronts us unless we give a name to the root of the evils which afflict us.

---

[65] Apostolic Exhortation *Reconciliatio et Paenitentia* (2 December 1984), 16: "Whenever the Church speaks of *situations* of sin, or when she condemns as *social sins* certain situations or the collective behaviour of certain social groups, big or small, or even of whole nations and blocs of nations, she knows and she proclaims that such cases of *social sin* are the result of the accumulation and concentration of many *personal sins.* It is a case of the very personal sins of those who cause or support evil or who exploit it; of those who are in a position to avoid, eliminate or at least limit certain social evils but who fail to do so out of laziness, fear or the conspiracy of silence, through secret complicity or indifference; of those who take refuge in the supposed impossibility of changing the world, and also of those who sidestep the effort and sacrifice required, producing specious reasons of a higher order. The real responsibility, then, lies with individuals. A situation— or likewise an institution, a structure, society itself — is not in itself the subject of moral acts. Hence a situation cannot in itself be good or bad": *AAS* 77 (1985), p. 217.

One can certainly speak of "selfishness" and of "shortsightedness", of "mistaken political calculations" and "imprudent economic decisions". And in each of these evaluations one hears an echo of an ethical and moral nature. Man's condition is such that a more profound analysis of individuals' actions and omissions cannot be achieved without implying, in one way or another, judgments or references of an ethical nature.

This evaluation is in itself *positive,* especially if it is completely consistent and if it is based on faith in God and on his law, which commands what is good and forbids evil.

In this consists the difference between socio-political analysis and formal reference to "sin" and the "structures of sin". According to this latter viewpoint, there enter in the will of the Triune God, his plan for humanity, his justice and his mercy. The God who is *rich in mercy, the Redeemer of man, the Lord and giver of life,* requires from people clearcut attitudes which express themselves also in actions or omissions towards one's neighbour. We have here a reference to the "second tablet" of the Ten Commandments (cf. *Ex* 20:12-17; *Dt* 5:16-21). Not to observe these is to offend God and hurt one's neighbour, and to introduce into the world influences and obstacles which go far beyond the actions and the brief lifespan of an individual. This also involves interference in the process of the development of peoples, the

70

delay or slowness of which must be judged also in this light.

37. This *general analysis,* which is religious in nature, can be supplemented by *a number of particular considerations* to demonstrate that among the actions and attitudes opposed to the will of God, the good of neighbour and the "structures" created by them, two are very typical: on the one hand, the *all-consuming desire for profit,* and on the other, *the thirst for power,* with the intention of imposing one's will upon others. In order to characterize better each of these attitudes, one can add the expression: "at any price". In other words, we are faced with the *absolutizing* of human attitudes with all its possible consequences.

Since these attitudes can exist independently of each other, they can be separated; however in today's world both are *indissolubly united,* with one or the other predominating.

Obviously, not only individuals fall victim to this double attitude of sin; nations and blocs can do so too. And this favours even more the introduction of the "structures of sin" of which I have spoken. If certain forms of modern "imperialism" were considered in the light of these moral criteria, we would see that hidden behind certain decisions, apparently inspired only by economics or politics, are real forms of idolatry: of money, ideology, class, technology.

I have wished to introduce this type of

analysis above all in order to point out the true *nature* of the evil which faces us with respect to the development of peoples: it is a question of a *moral evil,* the fruit of *many sins* which lead to "structures of sin". To diagnose the evil in this way is to identify precisely, on the level of human conduct, *the path to be followed* in order *to overcome it.*

38.   This path is *long and complex,* and what is more it is constantly threatened because of the intrinsic frailty of human resolutions and achievements, and because of the *mutability* of very unpredictable external circumstances. Nevertheless, one must have the courage to set out on this path, and, where some steps have been taken or a part of the journey made, the courage to go on to the end.

In the context of these reflections, the decision to set out or to continue the journey involves, above all, a *moral* value which men and women of faith recognize as a demand of God's will, the only true foundation of an absolutely binding ethic.

One would hope that also men and women without an explicit faith would be convinced that the obstacles to integral development are not only economic but rest on *more profound attitudes* which human beings can make into absolute values. Thus one would hope that all those who, to some degree or other, are responsible for ensuring a "more human life" for their fellow human beings, whether or not they are inspired by a religious faith, will become fully aware of the urgent need to *change* the *spiritual attitudes* which define each individual's relationship with self, with neighbour, with even the remotest human communities, and with nature itself; and all of this in view of higher values such as the *common good* or, to quote the felicitous expression of the Encyclical *Populorum Progressio,* the full development "of the whole individual and of all people".[66]

For *Christians,* as for all who recognize the precise theological meaning of the word "sin", a change of behaviour or mentality or mode of existence is called "conversion", to use the language of the Bible (cf. *Mk* 13: 3, 5; *Is* 30: 15). This conversion specifically entails a relationship to God, to the sin committed, to its consequences and hence to one's neighbour, either an individual or a community. It is God, in "whose hands are the hearts of the powerful" [67] and the hearts of all, who according to his own promise and by the power of his Spirit can transform "hearts of stone" into "hearts of flesh" (cf. *Ezek* 36: 26).

On the path towards the desired conversion, towards the overcoming of the moral obstacles to development, it is already possible to point to the *positive* and *moral value* of the growing

[66] Encyclical Letter *Populorum Progressio,* 42: *loc. cit.,* p. 278.
[67] Cf. *Liturgia Horarum,* Feria III Hebdomadae III^ac Temporis per annum, Preces ad Vesperas.

awareness of *interdependence* among individuals and nations. The fact that men and women in various parts of the world feel personally affected by the injustices and violations of human rights committed in distant countries, countries which perhaps they will never visit, is a further sign of a reality transformed into *awareness,* thus acquiring a *moral* connotation.

It is above all a question of *interdependence,* sensed as a *system determining* relationships in the contemporary world, in its economic, cultural, political and religious elements, and accepted as a *moral category.* When interdependence becomes recognized in this way, the correlative response as a moral and social attitude, as a "virtue", is *solidarity.* This then is not a feeling of vague compassion or shallow distress at the misfortunes of so many people, both near and far. On the contrary, it is *a firm and persevering determination* to commit oneself to the *common good;* that is to say to the good of all and of each individual, because we are *all* really responsible *for all.* This determination is based on the *solid* conviction that what is hindering full development is that desire for profit and that thirst for power already mentioned. These attitudes and "structures of sin" are only conquered—presupposing the help of divine grace— by a *diametrically opposed attitude:* a commitment to the good of one's neighbour with the readiness, in the Gospel sense, to "lose oneself" for the sake of the other instead of exploiting him, and to "serve him" instead of oppressing him for one's own advantage (cf. *Mt* 10:40-42; 20:25; *Mk* 10:42-45; *Lk* 22:25-27).

39. The exercise of solidarity *within each society* is valid when its members recognize one another as persons. Those who are more influential, because they have a greater share of goods and common services, should feel *responsible* for the weaker and be ready to share with them all they possess. Those who are weaker, for their part, in the same spirit of *solidarity,* should not adopt a purely *passive* attitude or one that is *destructive* of the social fabric, but, while claiming their legitimate rights, should do what they can for the good of all. The intermediate groups, in their turn, should not selfishly insist on their particular interests, but respect the interests of others.

Positive signs in the contemporary world are the *growing awareness* of the solidarity of the poor among themselves, their *efforts to support one another,* and their *public demonstrations* on the social scene which, without recourse to violence, present their own needs and rights in the face of the inefficiency or corruption of the public authorities. By virtue of her own evangelical duty the Church feels called to take her stand beside the poor, to discern the justice of their requests, and to help satisfy them, without losing sight of the good of groups in the context of the common good.

The same criterion is applied by analogy in international relationships. Interdependence must be transformed into *solidarity*, based upon the principle that the goods of creation *are meant for all*. That which human industry produces through the processing of raw materials, with the contribution of work, must serve equally for the good of all.

Surmounting every type of *imperialism* and determination to preserve their *own hegemony*, the stronger and richer nations must have a sense of moral *responsibility* for the other nations, so that a *real international system* may be established which will rest on the foundation of the *equality* of all peoples and on the necessary respect for their legitimate differences. The economically weaker countries, or those still at subsistence level, must be enabled, with the assistance of other peoples and of the international community, to make a contribution of their own to the common good with their treasures of *humanity* and *culture*, which otherwise would be lost for ever.

Solidarity helps us to see the "other"— whether a *person, people or nation*—not just as some kind of instrument, with a work capacity and physical strength to be exploited at low cost and then discarded when no longer useful, but as our "neighbour", a "helper" (cf. *Gen* 2:18-20), to be made a sharer, on a par with ourselves, in the banquet of life to which all are equally invited by God. Hence the importance of reawakening the *religious awareness* of individuals and peoples.

Thus the exploitation, oppression and annihilation of others are excluded. These facts, in the present division of the world into opposing blocs, combine to produce the *danger of war* and an excessive preoccupation with personal security, often to the detriment of the autonomy, freedom of decision, and even the territorial integrity of the weaker nations situated within the so-called "areas of influence" or "safety belts".

The "structures of sin" and the sins which they produce are likewise radically opposed to *peace and development,* for development, *in the* familiar expression of Pope Paul's Encyclical, is "the new name for peace".[68]

In this way, the solidarity which we propose is the *path to peace and at the same time to development.* For world peace is inconceivable unless the world's leaders come to recognize that *interdependence* in itself demands the abandonment of the politics of blocs, the sacrifice of all forms of economic, military or political imperialism, and the transformation of mutual distrust into *collaboration.* This is precisely the *act proper* to solidarity among individuals and nations.

The motto of the pontificate of my esteemed predecessor Pius XII was *Opus iustitiae pax,* peace as the fruit of justice. Today one could say, with the same exactness and the same power

[68] Encyclical Letter *Populorum Progressio,* 87: *loc. cit.,* p. 299.

of biblical inspiration (cf. *Is* 32:17; *Jas* 3:18): *Opus solidaritatis pax,* peace as the fruit of solidarity.

The goal of peace, so desired by everyone, will certainly be achieved through the putting into effect of social and international justice, but also through the practice of the virtues which favour togetherness, and which teach us to live in unity, so as to build in unity, by giving and receiving, a new society and a better world.

40.   *Solidarity* is undoubtedly a *Christian virtue.* In what has been said so far it has been possible to identify many points of contact between solidarity and *charity,* which is the distinguishing mark of Christ's disciples (cf. *Jn* 13:35).

In the light of faith, solidarity seeks to go beyond itself, to take on the *specifically Christian* dimensions of total gratuity, forgiveness and reconciliation. One's neighbour is then not only a human being with his or her own rights and a fundamental equality with everyone else, but becomes the *living image* of God the Father, redeemed by the blood of Jesus Christ and placed under the permanent action of the Holy Spirit. One's neighbour must therefore be loved, even if an enemy, with the same love with which the Lord loves him or her; and for that person's sake one must be ready for sacrifice, even the ultimate one: to lay down one's life for the brethren (cf. *1 Jn* 3:16).

At that point, awareness of the common fatherhood of God, of the brotherhood of all in Christ—"children in the Son"—and of the presence and life-giving action of the Holy Spirit will bring to our vision of the world *a new criterion* for interpreting it. Beyond human and natural bonds, already so close and strong, there is discerned in the light of faith a new *model* of the *unity* of the human race, which must ultimately inspire our *solidarity*. This supreme *model of unity,* which is a reflection of the intimate life of God, one God in three Persons, is what we Christians mean by the word "*communion*". This specifically Christian communion, jealously preserved, extended and enriched with the Lord's help, is the *soul* of the Church's vocation to be a "sacrament", in the sense already indicated.

Solidarity therefore must play its part in the realization of this divine plan, both on the level of individuals and on the level of national and international society. The "evil mechanisms" and "structures of sin" of which we have spoken can be overcome only through the exercise of the human and Christian solidarity to which the Church calls us and which she tirelessly promotes. Only in this way can such positive energies be fully released for the benefit of development and peace.

Many of the Church's canonized saints offer a *wonderful witness* of such solidarity and can serve as examples in the present difficult circumstances. Among them I wish to recall Saint Peter Claver and his service to the slaves at Cartagena de Indias, and Saint Maximilian Maria Kolbe who offered his life in place of a prisoner unknown to him in the concentration camp at Auschwitz.

VI

SOME PARTICULAR GUIDELINES

41. The Church does not have *technical solutions* to offer for the problem of under-development as such, as Pope Paul VI already affirmed in his Encyclical.[69] For the Church does not propose economic and political systems or programmes, nor does she show preference for one or the other, provided that human dignity is properly respected and promoted, and provided she herself is allowed the room she needs to exercise her ministry in the world.

But the Church is an "expert in humanity",[70] and this leads her necessarily to extend her religious mission to the various fields in which men and women expend their efforts in search of the always relative happiness which is possible in this world, in line with their dignity as persons.

Following the example of my predecessors, I must repeat that whatever affects the dignity of individuals and peoples, such as authentic development, cannot be reduced to a "technical"

[69] Cf. *ibid.*, 13; 81: *loc. cit.*, pp. 263 f.; 296 f.
[70] Cf. *ibid.*, 13: *loc. cit.*, p. 263.

81

problem. If reduced in this way, development would be emptied of its true content, and this would be an act of *betrayal* of the individuals and peoples whom development is meant to serve.

This is why the Church has *something to say* today, just as twenty years ago, and also in the future, about the nature, conditions, requirements and aims of authentic development, and also about the obstacles which stand in its way. In doing so the Church fulfils her mission to *evangelize,* for she offers her *first* contribution to the solution of the urgent problem of development when she proclaims the truth about Christ, about herself and about man, applying this truth to a concrete situation.[71]

As her *instrument* for reaching this goal, the Church uses her *social doctrine.* In today's difficult situation, a *more exact awareness and a wider diffusion* of the "set of principles for reflection, criteria for judgment and directives for action" proposed by the Church's teaching[72] would be of great help in promoting both the correct definition of the problems being faced and the best solution to them.

It will thus be seen at once that the questions

---

[71] Cf. Address at the Opening of the Third General Conference of the Latin American Bishops (28 January 1979): *AAS* 71 (1979), pp. 189-196.

[72] CONGREGATION FOR THE DOCTRINE OF THE FAITH, Instruction on Christian Freedom and Liberation *Libertatis Conscientia* (22 March 1986), 72: *AAS* 79 (1987) p. 586; PAUL VI, Apostolic Letter *Octogesima Adveniens* (14 May 1971), 4: *AAS* 63 (1971) pp. 403 f.

facing us are above all moral questions; and that neither the analysis of the problem of development as such nor the means to overcome the present difficulties can ignore this essential dimension.

The Church's social doctrine *is not* a "third way" between *liberal capitalism* and *Marxist collectivism,* nor even a possible alternative to other solutions less radically opposed to one another: rather, it constitutes a *category of its own.* Nor is it an *ideology,* but rather the *accurate formulation* of the results of a careful reflection on the complex realities of human existence, in society and in the international order, in the light of faith and of the Church's tradition. Its main aim is to *interpret* these realities, determining their conformity with or divergence from the lines of the Gospel teaching on man and his vocation, a vocation which is at once earthly and transcendent; its aim is thus *to guide* Christian behaviour. It therefore belongs to the field, not of *ideology,* but of *theology* and particularly of moral theology.

The teaching and spreading of her social doctrine are part of the Church's evangelizing mission. And since it is a doctrine aimed at guiding *people's behaviour,* it consequently gives rise to a "commitment to justice", according to each individual's role, vocation and circumstances.

The *condemnation* of evils and injustices is also part of that *ministry of evangelization* in the social field which is an aspect of the Church's *prophetic role.* But it should be made clear that *proclamation* is always more important than *condemnation,* and the latter cannot ignore the former, which gives it true solidity and the force of higher motivation.

42. Today more than in the past, the Church's social doctrine must be open to an *international outlook,* in line with the Second Vatican Council,[73] the most recent Encyclicals,[74] and particularly in line with the Encyclical which we are commemorating.[75] It will not be superfluous therefore to re-examine and further clarify in this light the characteristic themes and guidelines dealt with by the Magisterium in recent years.

Here I would like to indicate one of them: the *option* or *love of preference* for the poor. This is an option, or a *special form* of primacy in the exercise of Christian charity, to which the whole tradition of the Church bears witness. It affects the life of each Christian inasmuch as he or she seeks to imitate the life of Christ, but it applies equally to our *social responsibilities*

[73] Cf. Pastoral Constitution on the Church in the Modern World *Gaudium et Spes,* Part II, Ch. V, Section 2: "Building up the International Community", 83-90.

[74] Cf. JOHN XXIII, Encyclical Letter *Mater et Magistra* (15 May 1961): *AAS* 53 (1961), p. 440; Encyclical Letter *Pacem in Terris* (11 April 1963), Part IV: *AAS* 55 (1963) pp. 291-296; PAUL VI, Apostolic Letter *Octogesima Adveniens* (14 May 1971), 2-4: *AAS* 63 (1971), pp. 402-404.

[75] Cf. Encyclical Letter *Populorum Progressio,* 3; 9: *loc. cit,.,* pp. 258; 261.

and hence to our manner of living, and to the logical decisions to be made concerning the ownership and use of goods.

Today, furthermore, given the worldwide dimension which the social question has assumed,[76] this love of preference for the poor, and the decisions which it inspires in us, cannot but embrace the immense multitudes of the hungry, the needy, the homeless, those without medical care and, above all, those without hope of a better future. It is impossible not to take account of the existence of these realities. To ignore them would mean becoming like the "rich man" who pretended not to know the beggar Lazarus lying at his gate (cf. *Lk* 16: 19-31).[77]

Our *daily life* as well as our decisions in the political and economic fields must be marked by these realities. Likewise the *leaders* of nations and the heads of *International Bodies,* while they are obliged always to keep in mind the true human dimension as a priority in their development plans, should not forget to give precedence to the phenomenon of growing poverty. Unfortunately, instead of becoming fewer the poor are becoming more numerous, not only in less developed countries but—and this seems no

[76] *Ibid.,* 3: *loc. cit.,* p. 258.
[77] Encyclical Letter *Populorum Progressio,* 47: *loc. cit.,* p. 280; CONGREGATION FOR THE DOCTRINE OF THE FAITH, Instruction on Christian Freedom and Liberation *Libertatis Conscientia* (22 March 1986), 68: *AAS* 79 (1987) pp. 583 f.

less scandalous—in the more developed ones too.

It is necessary to state once more the characteristic principle of Christian social doctrine: the goods of this world are *originally meant for all*.[78] The right to private property is *valid and necessary,* but it does not nullify the value of this principle. Private property, in fact, is under a "social mortgage",[79] which means that it has an intrinsically social function, based upon and justified precisely by the principle of the universal destination of goods. Likewise, in this concern for the poor, one must not overlook that *special form of poverty* which consists in being deprived of fundamental human rights, in particular the right to religious freedom and also the right to freedom of economic initiative.

43. The motivating concern for the poor —who are, in the very meaningful term, "the Lord's poor" [80]—must be translated at all levels

[78] Cf. Second Vatican Ecumenical Council, Pastoral Constitution on the Church in the Modern World *Gaudium et Spes,* 69; Paul VI, Encyclical Letter *Populorum Progressio,* 22: *loc. cit.,* p. 268; Congregation for the Doctrine of the Faith, Instruction on Christian Freedom and Liberation *Libertatis Conscientia* (22 March 1986), 90: *AAS* 79 (1987), p. 594; St Thomas Aquinas, *Summa Theol.* II^a II^{ae}, q. 66, art. 2.

[79] Cf. Address at the Opening of the Third General Conference of the Latin American Bishops (28 January 1979): *AAS* 71 (1979), pp. 189-196; *Ad Limina* Address to a group of Polish Bishops, (17 December 1987), 6: *L'Osservatore Romano,* 18 December 1987.

[80] Because the Lord wished to identify himself with them (*Mt* 25:31-46) and takes special care of them (cf. *Ps* 12 [11]: 6; *Lk* 1:52 f.).

into concrete actions, until it decisively attains a series of necessary reforms. Each local situation will show what reforms are most urgent and how they can be achieved. But those demanded by the situation of international imbalance, as already described, must not be forgotten.

In this respect I wish to mention specifically: the *reform of the international trade system,* which is mortgaged to protectionism and increasing bilateralism; the *reform of the world monetary and financial system,* today recognized as inadequate; the *question of technological exchanges* and their proper use; the *need* for a *review of the structure of the existing International Organizations,* in the framework of an international juridical order.

The *international trade system* today frequently discriminates against the products of the young industries of the developing countries and discourages the producers of raw materials. There exists, too, a kind of *international division of labour,* whereby the low-cost products of certain countries which lack effective labour laws or which are too weak to apply them are sold in other parts of the world at considerable profit for the companies engaged in this form of production, which knows no frontiers.

The *world monetary and financial system* is marked by an excessive fluctuation of exchange rates and interest rates, to the detriment of the balance of payments and the debt situation of the poorer countries.

Forms of technology and their transfer constitute today one of the major problems of international exchange and of the grave damage deriving therefrom. There are quite frequent cases of developing countries being denied needed forms of technology or sent useless ones.

In the opinion of many, the *International Organizations* seem to be at a stage of their existence when their operating methods, operating costs and effectiveness need careful review and possible correction. Obviously, such a delicate process cannot be put into effect without the collaboration of all. This presupposes the overcoming of political rivalries and the renouncing of all desire to manipulate these Organizations, which exist solely for *the common good*.

The existing Institutions and Organizations have worked well for the benefit of peoples. Nevertheless, humanity today is in a new and more difficult phase of its genuine development. It needs a *greater degree of international ordering,* at the service of the societies, economies and cultures of the whole world.

44.   Development demands above all a spirit of initiative on the part of the countries which need it.[81]   Each of them must act in accordance

[81] Encyclical Letter *Populorum Progressio,* 55: *loc. cit.,* p. 284: "these are the men and women that need to be helped, that need to be convinced to take into their own hands their development, gradually acquiring the means"; cf. Pastoral Constitution on the Church in the Modern World *Gaudium et Spes,* 86.

with its own responsibilities, *not expecting everything* from the more favoured countries, and acting in collaboration with others in the same situation. Each must discover and use to the best advantage its *own area of freedom.* Each must make itself capable of initiatives responding to its own needs as a society. Each must likewise realize its true needs as well as the rights and duties which oblige it to respond to them. The development of peoples begins and is most appropriately accomplished in the dedication of each people to its own development, in collaboration with others.

It is important then that as far as possible *the developing nations themselves* should favour the *self-affirmation* of each citizen, through access to a wider culture and a free flow of information. Whatever promotes *literacy* and the *basic education* which completes and deepens it is a direct contribution to true development, as the Encyclical *Populorum Progressio* proposed.[82] These goals are still far from being reached in so many parts of the world.

In order to take this path, *the nations themselves* will have to identify their own *priorities* and clearly recognize their own needs, according to the particular conditions of their people, their geographical setting and their cultural traditions.

---

[82] Encyclical Letter *Populorum Progressio,* 35: *loc. cit.,* p. 274: "Basic education is the first objective of a plan of development".

Some nations will have to increase *food production,* in order to have always available what is needed for subsistence and daily life. In the modern world—where starvation claims so many victims, especially among the very young—there are examples of not particularly developed nations which have nevertheless achieved the goal of *food self-sufficiency* and have even become food exporters.

Other nations need to reform certain unjust structures, and in particular their *political institutions,* in order to replace corrupt, dictatorial and authoritarian forms of government by *democratic* and *participatory* ones. This is a process which we hope will spread and grow stronger. For the "health" of a political community—as expressed in the free and responsible participation of all citizens in public affairs, in the rule of law and in respect for and promotion of human rights—is the *necessary condition and sure guarantee* of the development of "the whole individual and of all people".

45.   None of what has been said can be achieved *without the collaboration of all*—especially the international community—in the framework of a *solidarity* which includes everyone, beginning with the most neglected. But the developing nations themselves have the duty to practice *solidarity among themselves* and with the neediest countries of the world.

It is desirable, for example, that nations of the *same geographical area* should establish *forms of cooperation* which will make them less dependent on more powerful producers; they should open their frontiers to the products of the area; they should examine how their products might complement one another; they should combine in order to set up those services which each one separately is incapable of providing; they should extend cooperation to the monetary and financial sector.

Interdependence is already a reality in many of these countries. To acknowledge it, in such a way as to make it more operative, represents an alternative to excessive dependence on richer and more powerful nations, as part of the hoped-for development, without opposing anyone, but discovering and making best use of the country's *own potential.* The developing countries belonging to one geographical area, especially those included in the term "South", can and ought to set up *new regional organizations* inspired by criteria of *equality, freedom and participation* in the comity of nations—as is already happening with promising results.

An essential condition for global *solidarity* is autonomy and free self-determination, also within associations such as those indicated. But at the same time solidarity demands a readiness to accept the sacrifices necessary for the good of the whole world community.

VII

CONCLUSION

46.   Peoples and individuals aspire to be free:
their search for full development signals their
desire to overcome the many obstacles preventing
them from enjoying a "more human life".

Recently, in the period following the publication of the Encyclical *Populorum Progressio,* a
new way of confronting the problems of poverty
and underdevelopment has spread in some areas
of the world, especially in Latin America. This
approach makes *liberation* the fundamental category and the first principle of action. The positive values, as well as the deviations and risks
of deviation, which are damaging to the faith
and are connected with this form of theological
reflection and method, have been appropriately
pointed out by the Church's Magisterium.[83]

It is fitting to add that the aspiration to
freedom from all forms of slavery affecting the

---

[83] Cf. CONGREGATION FOR THE DOCTRINE OF THE FAITH, Instruction on Certain Aspects of the "Theology of Liberation" *Libertatis Conscientia* (6 August 1984), Introduction: *AAS* 76 (1984),
pp. 876 f.

individual and society is something *noble* and *legitimate*. This in fact is the purpose of development, or rather liberation and development, taking into account the intimate connection between the two.

Development which is merely economic is incapable of setting man free; on the contrary, it will end by enslaving him further. Development that does not include the *cultural, transcendent and religious dimensions* of man and society, to the extent that it does not recognize the existence of such dimensions and does not endeavour to direct its goals and priorities towards the same, is *even less* conducive to authentic liberation. Human beings are totally free only when they are completely *themselves,* in the fullness of their rights and duties. The same can be said about society as a whole.

The principal obstacle to be overcome on the way to authentic liberation is *sin* and the *structures* produced by sin as it multiplies and spreads.[84]

The freedom with which Christ has set us free (cf. *Gal* 5:1) encourages us to become the *servants* of all. Thus the process of *development* and *liberation* takes concrete shape in the exercise of *solidarity,* that is to say in the love and service of neighbour, especially of the poorest:

[84] Cf. Apostolic Exhortation *Reconciliatio et Paenitentia* (2 December 1984), 16: *AAS* 77 (1985), pp. 213-217; CONGREGATION FOR THE DOCTRINE OF THE FAITH, Instruction on Christian Freedom and Liberation *Libertatis Conscientia* (22 March 1986), 38; 42: *AAS* 79 (1987), pp. 569; 571.

"For where truth and love are missing, the process of liberation results in the death of a freedom which will have lost all support".[85]

47. In the context of the *sad experiences* of recent years and of the *mainly negative picture* of the present moment, the Church must strongly affirm the *possibility* of overcoming the obstacles which, by excess or by defect, stand in the way of development. And she must affirm her confidence in a *true liberation*. Ultimately, this confidence and this possibility are based on the *Church's awareness* of the divine promise guaranteeing that our present history does not remain closed in upon itself but is open to the Kingdom of God.

The Church has *confidence also in man,* though she knows the evil of which he is capable. For she well knows that—in spite of the heritage of sin, and the sin which each one is capable of committing—there exist in the human person sufficient qualities and energies, a fundamental "goodness" (cf. *Gen* 1:31), because he is the image of the creator, placed under the redemptive influence of Christ, who "united himself in some fashion with every man",[86] and

[85] CONGREGATION FOR THE DOCTRINE OF THE FAITH, Instruction on Christian Freedom and Liberation *Libertatis Conscientia* (22 March 1986), 24: *AAS* 79 (1987), p. 564.
[86] Cf. Pastoral Constitution on the Church in the Modern World *Gaudium et Spes,* 22; JOHN PAUL II, Encyclical Letter *Redemptor Hominis* (4 March 1979), 8: *AAS* 71 (1979), p. 272.

because the efficacious action of the Holy Spirit "fills the earth" (*Wis* 1:7).

There is no justification then for despair or pessimism or inertia. Though it be with sorrow, it must be said that just as one may sin through selfishness and the desire for excessive profit and power, *one may also be found wanting* with regard to the urgent needs of multitudes of human beings submerged in conditions of underdevelopment, through *fear, indecision* and, basically, through *cowardice.* We are *all* called, indeed *obliged,* to face the *tremendous challenge* of the last decade of the second Millennium, also because the present dangers threaten everyone: a world economic crisis, a war without frontiers, without winners or losers. In the face of such a threat, the distinction between rich individuals and countries and poor individuals and countries *will have little value,* except that a greater responsibility rests on those who have more and can do more.

This is not however the *sole motive or even the most important one.* At stake is the *dignity of the human person,* whose *defence* and *promotion* have been entrusted to us by the Creator, and to whom the men and women at every moment of history are strictly and responsibly *in debt.* As many people are already more or less clearly aware, the present situation *does not seem to correspond to* this dignity. *Every individual* is called upon to play his or her part in this *peaceful* campaign, a campaign to be conducted by *peaceful* means, in order to secure *development in peace,* in order to safeguard nature itself and the world about us. The Church too feels profoundly involved in this enterprise, and she hopes for its ultimate success.

Consequently, following the example of Pope Paul VI with his Encyclical *Populorum Progressio,*[87] I wish *to appeal* with simplicity and humility to *everyone,* to all men and women without exception. I wish to ask them to be convinced of the seriousness of the present moment and of each one's individual responsibility, and to implement—by the way they live as individuals and as families, by the use of their resources, by their civic activity, by contributing to economic and political decisions and by personal commitment to national and international undertakings—the *measures* inspired by solidarity and love of preference for the poor. This is what is demanded by the present moment and above all by the very dignity of the human person, the indestructible image of God the Creator, which is *identical* in each one of us.

In this commitment, the sons and daughters of the Church must serve as examples and guides, for they are called upon, in conformity with the programme announced by Jesus himself in the synagogue at Nazareth, to "preach

[87] Encyclical Letter *Populorum Progressio,* 5: *loc. cit.,* p. 259: "We believe that all men of good will, together with our Catholic sons and daughters and our Christian brethren, can and should agree on this programme"; cf. also 81-83, 87: *loc. cit.,* pp. 296-298; 299.

good news to the poor ... to proclaim release to the captives and recovering of sight to the blind, to set at liberty those who are oppressed, to proclaim the acceptable year of the Lord" (*Lk* 4: 18-19). It is appropriate to emphasize the *preeminent role* that belongs to the *laity,* both men and women, as was reaffirmed in the recent Assembly of the Synod. It is their task to animate temporal realities with Christian commitment, by which they show that they are witnesses and agents of peace and justice.

I wish to address especially those who, through the Sacrament of Baptism and the profession of the same Creed, *share* a *real,* though imperfect, *communion* with us. I am certain that the concern expressed in this Encyclical as well as the motives inspiring it *will be familiar to them,* for these motives are inspired by the Gospel of Jesus Christ. We can find here a new invitation *to bear witness together* to our *common convictions* concerning the dignity of man, created by God, redeemed by Christ, made holy by the Spirit and called upon in this world to live a life in conformity with this dignity.

I likewise address this appeal to the Jewish people, who share with us the inheritance of Abraham, "our father in faith" (cf. *Rm* 4: 11 f.) [88] and the tradition of the Old Testament, as well as to the Muslims who, like us, believe

---

[88] Cf. SECOND VATICAN ECUMENICAL COUNCIL, Declaration on the Relationship of the Church to Non-Christian Religions, *Nostra Aetate,* 4.

in the just and merciful God. And I extend it to all the followers of *the world's great religions.*

The meeting held on 27 October last in Assisi, the city of Saint Francis, in order to pray for and commit ourselves to *peace*—each one in fidelity to his own religious profession—showed how much peace and, as its necessary condition, the development of the whole person and of all peoples, are also a *matter of religion,* and how the full achievement of both the one and the other depends on our *fidelity* to our vocation as men and women of faith. For it depends, above all, *on God.*

48. The Church well knows that *no temporal achievement* is to be identified with the Kingdom of God, but that all such achievements simply *reflect* and in a sense *anticipate* the glory of the Kingdom, the Kingdom which we await at the end of history, when the Lord will come again. But that expectation can never be an excuse for lack of concern for people in their concrete personal situations and in their social, national and international life, since the former is conditioned by the latter, especially today.

However imperfect and temporary are all the things that can and ought to be done through the combined efforts of everyone and through divine grace, at a given moment of history, in order to make people's lives "more human", nothing will be *lost* or *will have been in vain.* This is the teaching of the Second Vatican Council, in an enlightening passage of the Pastoral Constitution *Gaudium et Spes:* "When we have spread on earth the fruits of our nature and our enterprise—human dignity, fraternal communion, and freedom—according to the command of the Lord and in his Spirit, we will find them once again, cleansed this time from the stain of sin, illumined and transfigured, when Christ presents to his Father an eternal and universal kingdom ... here on earth that kingdom is already present in mystery".[89]

The Kingdom of God becomes *present* above all in the celebration of the *Sacrament of the Eucharist,* which is the Lord's Sacrifice. In that celebration the fruits of the earth and the work of human hands—the bread and wine—are transformed mysteriously, but really and substantially, through the power of the Holy Spirit and the words of the minister, *into the Body and Blood* of the Lord Jesus Christ, the Son of God and Son of Mary, through whom the *Kingdom of the Father* has been made present in our midst.

The goods of this world and the work of our hands—the bread and wine—serve for the coming of the *definitive Kingdom,* since the Lord, through his Spirit, takes them up into himself in order to offer himself to the Father and to offer us with himself in the renewal of his one Sacrifice, which anticipates God's Kingdom and proclaims its final coming.

[89] *Gaudium et Spes,* 39.

Thus the Lord *unites us with himself* through the Eucharist—Sacrament and Sacrifice—and he *unites us with himself and with one another* by a bond stronger than any natural union; and thus united, *he sends us* into the whole world to bear witness, through faith and works, to God's love, preparing the coming of his Kingdom and anticipating it, though in the obscurity of the present time.

All of us who take part in the Eucharist are called to discover, through this Sacrament, the profound *meaning* of our actions in the world in favour of development and peace; and to receive from it the strength to commit ourselves ever more generously, following the example of Christ, who in this Sacrament lays down his life for his friends (cf. *Jn* 15:13). Our personal commitment, like Christ's and in union with his, will not be in vain but certainly fruitful.

49. I have called the current *Marian* Year in order that the Catholic faithful may look more and more to Mary who goes before us on the pilgrimage of faith [90] and with maternal care intercedes for us before her Son, our Redeemer. I wish to *entrust to her* and to *her intercession* this *difficult moment* of the modern world, and the efforts that are being made and will be made, often with great suffering, in order to contribute

[90] Cf. SECOND VATICAN ECUMENICAL COUNCIL, Dogmatic Constitution on the Church *Lumen Gentium,* 58; JOHN PAUL II, Encyclical Letter *Redemptoris Mater* (25 March 1987), 5-6: *AAS* 79 (1987), pp. 365-367.

to the true development of peoples proposed and proclaimed by my predecessor Paul VI.

In keeping with Christian piety through the ages, we present to the Blessed Virgin difficult individual situations, so that she may place them before her Son, asking that he *alleviate and change* them. But we also present to her *social situations* and *the international crisis* itself, in their worrying aspects of poverty, unemployment, shortage of food, the arms race, contempt for human rights, and situations or dangers of conflict, partial or total. In a filial spirit we wish to place all this before her "eyes of mercy", repeating once more with faith and hope the ancient antiphon: "Holy Mother of God, despise not our petitions in our necessities, but deliver us always from all dangers, O glorious and blessed Virgin".

Mary most holy, our Mother and Queen, is the one who turns to her Son and says: "They have no more wine" (*Jn* 2:3). She is also the one who praises God the Father, because "he has put down the mighty from their thrones and exalted those of low degree; he has filled the hungry with good things, and the rich he has sent empty away" (*Lk* 1:52-53). Her maternal concern extends to the *personal* and *social* aspects of people's life on earth.[91]

[91] Cf. PAUL VI, Apostolic Exhortation *Marialis Cultus* (2 February 1974), 37: *AAS* 66 (1974), pp. 148 f.; JOHN PAUL II, Homily at the Shrine of Our Lady of Zapopan, Mexico (30 January 1979), 4: *AAS* 71 (1979), p. 230.

Before the Most Blessed Trinity, I entrust to Mary all that I have written in this Encyclical, and I invite all to reflect and actively commit themselves to promoting the true development of peoples, as the prayer of the Mass for this intention states so well: "Father, you have given all peoples one common origin, and your will is to gather them as one family in yourself. Fill the hearts of all with the fire of your love, and the desire to ensure justice for all their brothers and sisters. By sharing the good things you give us may we secure justice and equality for every human being, an end to all division and a human society built on love and peace".[92]

This, in conclusion, is what I ask in the name of all my brothers and sisters, to whom I send a special blessing as a sign of greeting and good wishes.

Given in Rome, at Saint Peter's, on 30 December of the year 1987, the tenth of my Pontificate.

Joannes Paulus pp. II

---

[92] Collect of the Mass "For the Development of Peoples": *Missale Romanum*, ed. typ. altera, 1975, p. 820.